CORRUPT CITIES

A PRACTICAL GUIDE TO CURE AND PREVENTION

ROBERT KLITGAARD

RONALD MACLEAN-ABAROA

H. LINDSEY PARRIS

INSTITUTE FOR CONTEMPORARY STUDIES
OAKLAND, CALIFORNIA

Washington, DC USA
Visit the World Bank Institute's Governance and Anti-Corruption Internet site:
http://www.worldbank.org/wbi/governance/

This book is a publication of the Institute for Contemporary Studies (ICS), a non-profit, nonpartisan public policy research organization, and the World Bank Institute, the client and staff training arm of the World Bank. The analyses, conclusions, and opinions expressed in this publication are those of the authors and not necessarily those of ICS, the World Bank, or their officers, their directors, or others associated with, or funding, their work.

Executive offices of ICS are located at ICS Press, Latham Square, 1611 Telegraph Avenue, Suite 406, Oakland, CA 94612. Tel.: (510) 238-5010; Fax: (510) 238-8440; Internet: www.icspress.com; Email: mail@icspress.com. For book orders and catalog requests, call toll free in the United States: (800) 326-0263. Outside the United States, call (717) 325-5686.

The World Bank Institute is located at World Bank headquarters, 1818 H Street, N.W., Washington, DC 20433 USA. Tel.: (202) 458-2498; Governance and Anti-Corruption Internet site: http://www.worldbank.org/wbi/governance/
email: wbi_infoline@worldbank.org.

Special thanks is given to the Asia Foundation whose leadership made this book possible.

Cover and interior design by Rohani Design, Edmonds, WA. Book set in Garamond by Rohani Design.

0 9 8 7 6 5 4 3 2 1

Library of Congress Cataloging-in-Publication Data

Klitgaard, Robert E.

Corrupt cities : a practical guide to cure and prevention / Robert Klitgaard, Ronald MacLean-Abaroa, H. Lindsey Parris.

p. cm.

Includes index.

ICS: ISBN 1-55815-511-2

WBI: ISBN 0-8213-4600-8

1. Municipal government. 2. Political corruption. I. Title. II. MacLean-Abaroa, Ronald. III. Parris, H. Lindsey.

JS231.K58 2000

353.4'6214'0973 21—dc21 99-044544

Contents

Boxes

Institute for Contemporary Studies Foreword

Corruption has been with us since the beginning of human organization. It has always been part of our collective activities. Yet one cannot be complacent about corruption because it eats not only at the economic fabric of society but also at the moral foundations of order.

One is jolted out of complacency when one reads that much of the devastation caused by the recent earthquake in Turkey was a result of widespread corruption between the construction industry and government officials. Yet most of the time we do not see corruption or we wish to ignore it. Part of the problem in seeing corruption is that it operates best under the cloak of secrecy. Aristotle noted another part of the problem when he stated, "What is most common to the greatest number has least care bestowed upon it." Even today, most corruption still takes place in public places and we must build stronger incentives to reduce it.

Yet powerful new incentives have developed that hold great promise of subjecting corrupt practices to public scrutiny. The information age is providing citizens and nongovernmental organizations with powerful organizing tools and information to combat local corruption. Likewise, the global economy puts tremendous pressure on local governments to rid themselves of factors that reduce their competitiveness. Corruption is clearly a factor that can and does reduce the attractiveness of one community over another.

Without the tools to utilize it productively, information has little value. This book provides the indispensable set of tools. Elected officials, citizens, and public administrators can use these tools to determine where corruption is taking place and its root causes. Here the authors provide sage advice: Focus on the institutions that create the incentives for corruption rather than on the character of those committing the acts of corruption. Why? Because if the institutions, which create the incentives, are not changed, the next occupants of these positions will likely be just as corrupt as their predecessors. Finally, the authors provide concrete examples of successful efforts to fight corruption, including ways to involve citizens in the process.

Corrupt Cities also has a valuable role to play in teaching students how to analyze complex social systems. By focusing on the interrelationship between institution and character, the authors provide students with valuable tools to understand how these two critical components of human society blend and work together. To focus only on character or institutions is to miss half the dynamics of human order.

Robert B. Hawkins, Jr.
President
Institute for Contemporary Studies

World Bank Institute Foreword

The movement toward decentralization, accountability, and democratic forms of government at the local level is gathering momentum. In this context, the enormous costs of corruption are being explicitly recognized, as is the urgent need to correct governmental malfeasance. Corruption is an entrenched symptom of misgovernance often reflected in patronage, red tape, ineffective revenue-generating agencies, large scale bribery in procurement, and failure to deliver services to city dwellers. But when local officials in charge of public resources are accountable to their citizens, decisionmaking can become participatory. In turn, a participatory process can be the cornerstone of a subnational strategy to reform "sick" institutions and improve the welfare of city dwellers.

Corrupt Cities is an important contribution to this emerging field, addressing the historical, traditional, and cultural contexts that create perverse incentives for corruption to exist. At the same time, this book provides practical solutions and a set of incentives charting a path away from misgovernance toward effective local governance. The authors present case studies of both success and failure to underscore that addressing corruption is only an entry point to deeper public sector reforms. The book serves as a guide for local reformers and citizen groups intent on changing corrupt systems by introducing practical strategies to combat corruption and to reform local institutions. Practical tools and approaches are presented, including fiscal transfers, informatics to track public revenues and expenditures, simplified rules to improve the procurement process, diagnostics, and participatory techniques for developing and monitoring local budgets.

The challenge facing local governments is to develop innovative ways of building effective, accountable, and transparent systems. *Corrupt Cities* brings these innovations together in a systematic way, providing both a conceptual and a practical framework as well as an international perspective based on concrete country examples such as Hong Kong and La Paz. We learn about establishing a framework for policy formulation and implementation at the municipal level, anchored in modern management thinking. This framework ought to promote further innovative thinking and action by public reformers and citizen groups alike.

As part of its worldwide programs on anticorruption, governance, and municipal reform, the World Bank Institute (WBI) is learning and disseminating lessons about establishing credible and transparent municipal government. These programs are reaching out to a large and growing audience, including city managers in scores of countries around the world. The know-how in *Corrupt Cities* is already an integral part of this shared learning approach with city executives. We learn from this book and WBI's course participants that in spite of the apparent similarity of the problems and challenges across cities, each requires a particular approach grounded in the differing realities at the local level.

We also learn that in order to attain concrete and lasting results, a bold departure from traditional ways of doing business is often essential. In this context, strong political will, citizen voice, appropriate technical support, and a realistic long-term implementation strategy are central to success. Where there is integration among various factors significant results can be expected: informed knowledge (with action program formulation based on in-depth empirical evidence in each setting), coalition-building leading to collective action, and transparent political leadership at the local level. Cities implementing and sustaining ambitious governance reform programs benefiting the urban populace can expect to attract financial and human resources, and become showcases of exemplary practice to be emulated worldwide.

Daniel Kaufmann
Senior Manager
Governance, Regulation, and Finance Division
World Bank Institute

Preface

Preventing corruption helps to raise city revenues, improve service delivery, stimulate public confidence and participation, and win elections. This book is designed to help citizens and public officials diagnose, investigate, and prevent various kinds of corrupt and illicit behavior. It focuses on systematic corruption rather than the free-lance activity of a few lawbreakers, and emphasizes preventive measures rather than purely punitive or moralistic campaigns. Unlike many descriptive treatises on corruption, the book stresses practical steps.

This book offers examples of anti-corruption strategies that work. Even though corruption is a subject of passionate opinion and ethical freight, preventing it requires a strategy as coldly calculated as any other major innovation in a city's policy or management. A strategy must go beyond moralizing, legalisms, and the bromide that corruption would not exist if only we all fulfilled our obligations. It must transcend the reflex to install new rules, new regulations, and new layers of review.

The book also offers suggestions concerning *implementation* in difficult settings that may be characterized by political indifference, bureaucratic inertia, and citizen support not yet mobilized. We provide several frameworks for analysis and action, which we hope prove stimulating to policy makers and managers. Nonetheless, these frameworks do not pretend to tell mayors, city councilors, and top officials which buttons to push, policies to shift, systems to install, people to hire or fire, or even which forms of corruption should be dealt with first. The guidelines and examples do not compose a recipe applicable to each and every situation. They require careful reworking and adaptation to each locality's idiosyncrasies.

Readers may find that the book is at once humbler and bolder than many discussions of corruption, or indeed of city management. It humbly acknowledges that blueprints are not in the offing, that politics and practical questions of administration drive and constrain the possible lines of attack, and that what works in one city may not work in another. At the same time, it may be bold in asking readers to consider corruption through new lenses of economics and to eschew temporarily the accustomed lenses of morality and ethics. It considers, albeit schematically, what many treatises on management leave out, namely *tactics* for making good things happen even in corrupt settings. Also, our approach confides in the abilities of municipal officials to use the book to spark their creativity.

We try to place corruption in perspective. Corruption is not the only thing, or even the most important thing, about which municipal leaders should care. Today's cities must meet a multitude of objectives. They must provide services. They must empower citizens. They must work with the private sector in collegial relationships that would have been unusual or impossible a generation ago, and the relations often have a different goal: how to make cities into even more vibrant economic centers.

But tackling corruption in the right ways can be a means toward those broader aims. We do not recommend an approach to corruption that emphasizes more controls, more laws, and more bureaucracy. These can simply paralyze administration, and in some cases they can foster new and more deeply embedded varieties of corruption. Instead, especially in cases of systematic corruption, we advocate both restructuring city services and making institutional reforms that improve information and create new and more powerful incentives and disincentives. A major theme of this book is that *fighting corruption in the right ways can become a lever to achieve much broader ends, not only financial survival but also remaking the relationship between the citizen and local government.*

The book draws on both theoretical and practical contributions to preventing corruption, but its coverage does not aspire to the encyclopedic. The book does not intend to provide a compilation of what cities around the world have done and not done. Even the two case studies we analyze—Hong Kong in the 1970s and La Paz in the 1980s—are not presented in exhaustive detail. There is no magic wand here, and alas we suspect no such wand exists. Nonetheless, the approaches discussed in this book have helped officials in many countries analyze corruption, design strategies to reduce it, and implement those strategies in sometimes unfavorable political and administrative settings. Our message is optimistic. Corruption can in fact be prevented, even if never in this imperfect world eliminated.

The Importance of Corruption

WHAT IS "CORRUPTION" AND WHY IS IT HARMFUL?

Definition

Corruption is a universal problem, but around the world local governments seem particularly susceptible. For example, in Japan, according to one estimate, provincial governments have three times more officials than the national government but produce fifteen times the reported number of corruption cases and four times the number of arrested officials.[1] In New York City, the cost of past corruption in school construction alone is measured in the hundreds of millions of dollars.[2] Municipalities are often accused not only of mismanagement but of pouring public funds into private pockets. The charges are as varied as the activities of municipal authorities.

1. Bribes lead to the misallocation of subsidized housing.
2. Kickbacks to procurement officers mean that city contracts often go to unworthy firms.
3. City police departments sometimes look the other way at criminal offenses in exchange for a bribe.
4. Public property is used by city officials for private ends.

5. Permits and licenses are facilitated by speed money, and sometimes purchased for a bribe.
6. Bribery enables people to break safety, health, or other rules, thereby creating grave social risks.
7. City services may be unavailable without an illegal side payment.
8. Tax collectors may extort citizens, or even more often collude with taxpayers to abet evasion in exchange for a bribe.
9. Zoning decisions are influenced by corruption.

And so on: This list is not a complete typology of the corruption found in local governments around the world.

There are many definitions of corruption. Most broadly, corruption means the misuse of office for personal gain. The office is a position of trust, where one receives authority in order to act on behalf of an institution, be it private, public, or nonprofit. Corruption means charging an illicit price for a service or using the power of office to further illicit aims. Corruption can entail acts of omission or commission. It can involve legal activities or illegal ones. It can be internal to the organization (for example, embezzlement) or external to it (for example, extortion). The effects of various kinds of corruption vary widely. Although corrupt acts sometimes may result in a net social benefit, corruption usually leads to inefficiency, injustice, and inequity.[3]

Corrupt acts differ in extent as well as type. Some corruption is "free-lance," as individual officials or small groups of them try to take advantage of their monopoly powers to generate bribes. Sometimes, alas, corruption becomes systematic. Two authors have recently distinguished one sort of corruption that is analogous to a foul in sports, and another sort which is the breakdown

Box 1: Cities Vary

Some of the variations in the table below no doubt reflect differences in climate and geography, but some indicate differences in opportunities for corruption.

City	Construction permit delays, months	Construction time, months	Construction costs, US$/m2	House price to income ratio[a]	Journey to work, minutes	Squatter housing %[b]
Algiers	2	6	500	11.7	30	4
Bangkok	11	5	156	4.1	91	3
Beijing	24	17	90	14.8	25	3
Bogotá	36	6	171	6.5	90	8
Dar es Salaam	36	28	67	1.9	50	51
Hong Kong	2	30	641	7.4	45	3
Istanbul	2	16	110	5.0	40	51
Jakarta	28	2	65	3.5	40	3
Johannesburg	24	2	192	1.7	59	22
Karachi	na	12	87	1.9	na	44
Kingston	6	12	157	4.9	60	33
London	5	20	560	7.2	30	0
Madrid	8	18	510	3.7	33	0
Manila	36	3	148	2.6	30	6
Melbourne	36	3	383	3.9	25	0
New Delhi	36	24	94	7.7	59	17
Paris	2	8	990	4.2	40	0
Rio de Janeiro	6	18	214	2.3	107	16
Seoul	20	18	617	9.3	37	5
Singapore	2	9	749	2.8	30	1
Tokyo	8	12	2,604	11.6	40	0
Toronto	30	6	608	4.2	26	0
Washington, D.C.	36	4	500	3.9	29	0

Notes: na Not available. m^2 Meters squared.
a. Median price of house as a multiple of median annual income.
b. % of total housing stock occupying land illegally.
Source: The Economist, "A Survey of Cities," July 29, 1995, p. 8, citing unpublished data from the World Bank.

of the rules defining and enforcing fouls. In the latter case, the sports contest virtually collapses. Luis Moreno Ocampo calls it "hypercorruption." Herbert Werlin's label is "secondary corruption," and he compares it to alcoholism.[4]

Whatever the terminology, when corruption reaches this state, it is deadly; and this unfortunately is the situation in many cities around the world. Systematic corruption generates economic costs by distorting incentives, political costs by undermining institutions, and social costs by redistributing wealth and power toward the undeserving. When corruption undermines property rights, the rule of law, and incentives to invest, economic and political development are crippled. Corruption exists in all countries. But corruption tends to be more damaging to poor countries, where it can undermine property rights, the rule of law, and incentives to invest.

An Example

Few municipal officials will face situations as extreme as the one encountered by Ronald MacLean-Abaroa when he took over as mayor of La Paz, Bolivia. Yet as we have related his account to officials in other countries, listeners have responded with knowing smiles.

On September 13, 1985, I was sworn in as the first elected mayor of La Paz since 1948. I knew I would be facing a difficult task, but I never imagined how grave the situation was. I quickly discovered that I had better find someone to loan me money to survive into the next month, because my new salary was the equivalent of only US$45 per month. Not only that, I would find it almost impossible *to form my immediate staff since they would be paid even less. At the end of that day, I boarded the mayor's vehicle, a decrepit 1978 four-wheel drive, to return home, wondering if I had not fallen into a trap from which it was impossible to escape, short of resigning from my first elected office.*

The idea that radical change was essential turned out to be my savior. I was facing a limiting case. Bolivia was still in the midst of its worst economic crisis ever. The former president had had to cut his term short and leave office before being driven from it by the army, the people, or most likely a combination of both. Though an honest president, he was unable nonetheless to reverse the economic collapse. In August inflation had reached an estimated annual rate of 40,000 percent.

The next day I returned to my office, wondering where to start my reforms. The four-wheel drive had broken down, and I had to drive to work in my own car. While parking in front of city hall, I noticed that there among the crippled vehicles were two conspicuously fancy cars. One belonged, I later learned, to a foreign expert working with the municipality. The other, an elegant sedan, belonged to the cashier of city hall. I had my first hints of where the resources were.

The cashier was a fifth-class bureaucrat with a minimal salary who, I came to know, had the habit of changing several times a week which car he drove to work. He made no secret of his obvious prosperity. In fact he routinely offered loans to the impoverished municipal employees, including some of his superiors, charging a "competitive" weekly interest rate.

Later, up in my office, I developed a deep sense of isolation. Accustomed to working in the private sector, where I managed fair-sized mining companies, I was used to *working with a team. In my newly elected post, there was nothing that resembled a team. All the people I found looked and acted more like survivors of a wreck than anything else. The professional staff were earning an average of about US$30 per month. Many employees were anxiously seeking alternative sources of income to take home. Corruption, if not always on the scale of the cashier, was everywhere.*

Bolivia had just had a change of government at the national level, and the new administration was from a different party than my own. I would not be able to count on support from the national government, as had been customary in the recent past when mayors were appointed by the president and subsidized by the national treasury. New laws meant that cities were on their own financially, and I learned that in two weeks I would have to meet a payroll that was worth roughly 120 percent of the total monthly revenues of La Paz! Part of this was due to the hyperinflation and the changes in federal support. But part of it, maybe a lot of it, was due to corruption.

I found many signs of malignancy in the municipality. The degree of institutional decay was such that authority had virtually collapsed in the municipality. Everyone was looking to survive in terms of income generation, and therefore corruption was widespread. Tax collectors used techniques ranging from extortion to speed money to arrangements for lower taxes in exchange for a bribe. Property taxes were particularly vulnerable to collusion between taxpayers and corrupt officials. A new assessment was needed as the result of the hyperinflation; and a legion of municipal functionaries was ready to hit the streets, meet property owners, and "negotiate" a property value that would suit both owners and functionaries well, but one far below the true value. The result would be a tax saving for the property owners, particularly the rich; a bribe for the colluding functionary; and a city unable to provide services because it lacked even minimal resources.

The city government was in effect a huge "construction company" that wasn't constructing much. The city owned tractors, trucks, and all kinds of construction machinery. There were 4,000 city laborers, who were paid meager, fixed salaries and were only coming to work an average of five hours a day. Machinery was also used for a similar amount of time, rendering it extremely inefficient given its high capital cost. But I found that the use of gasoline, oil, and spare parts was abnormally high. Surely they were being sold in the black market, I thought, and soon this suspicion was sadly verified. New tires and expensive machinery parts such as fuel injectors, pumps, and Caterpillar parts were available for sale; and in exchange broken and used parts were "replaced" on the city's machinery.

Finally, there was the municipal police, a "soft police" that didn't conduct criminal investigations or carry arms but was responsible for regulating the informal sector, inspecting the markets for cleanliness, and keeping order among the city vendors. This, too, was a source of corruption, as the municipal police would extort money in exchange for letting vendors undertake both legal and illegal activities.

Faced with these overwhelming problems, Mayor MacLean-Abaroa thought briefly of resigning. Fortunately for La Paz, he did not; and instead as we shall see, he took strong actions to deal with these overwhelming problems. But many other municipal leaders in Bolivia and around the world have shied away from tackling corruption. In some cases this reluctance has been the consequence of complicity. In other cases mayors and city councilors have avoided the issue of corruption for other reasons. Some leaders have felt little electoral pressure, and some provincial and national governments have evinced little interest. In other cases local leaders have been unwilling to focus attention on corruption, fearing that even a relatively successful effort might nonetheless tar their administration with the label of "corrupt." Fighting corruption somehow implies that one is corrupt, and this in turn offers ammunition to one's opponents.

Finally, many leaders may simply have believed that little can be done about corruption. "How does one even get started on such a difficult set of issues?" they ask. The pages that follow try to provide some answers to this question.

Today signs indicate that the tide is turning. Around the world local and national elections feature corruption as a key issue. Gone are the days, it seems, when one could say what a mayor in Brazil bragged during his reelection campaign: "Robo mas faço obras" (loosely rendered: "Yes, I rob, but public works get done").

WHY IS CORRUPTION SUCH A SALIENT ISSUE TODAY?

Around the globe fighting corruption is surfacing now as a priority. Why? It is difficult to say, and several lines of explanation have been offered.

One possibility is that corruption has grown worse, leading to a wave of public outrage and new political resolve. But why might corruption have grown more severe? One line of argument cites the rapid rise of international trade and international communications, so that people are exposed to economic temptations as never before. Dipak Gyawali of the Royal Nepal Academy of Science and Technology believes that advertising has created new demands, and inflation-eroded salaries new perceived necessities, for corrupt behavior.[5] Another argument points to the democratic and economic reforms that have swept the world. In the long run, most people expect that political competition and economic liberalization will reduce corruption, because both tend to limit the arbitrary exercise of monopoly power. But in the short run, both democratic competition and new economic competition may have created opportunities for corruption by rapidly changing the accustomed rules of the game, leading to a kind of free-for-all with little enforcement. In many cases, corruption occurs because healthy policy changes are implemented through sick institutions, leading not to fair competition but to insider deals, political trafficking, and cities on the take.

It is also possible that the extent of corruption has not changed as much as our awareness and tolerance of it. We may more acutely perceive corruption's costs now that the Cold War has abated and economic policies and multiparty politics are roughly "gotten right." Or perhaps because political liberalization has granted new freedoms to document and complain about corruption, we are made more aware of it. Many countries enjoy a freer press and more international transfers of information than in the past; and both of these welcome conditions make it easier to report on corruption, even of the kinds that may also have existed in the past.

Another possibility is that people blame corruption for the fact that neither freer markets nor democratic reforms have yet lived up to expectations, in order to avoid admitting that those reforms may not work equally well under all settings. Corruption is the excuse of apologists for capitalism in the wake of capitalism's failures in the formerly Communist countries, some people have argued. They point to the seemingly sudden embrace of corruption as an issue by the formerly recalcitrant World Bank and International Monetary Fund. It is easier to criticize other people's corrupt implementation of one's strategies than to question the validity of those strategies themselves.

It is difficult to measure whether corruption is increasing or decreasing. Information about corruption is scarce and can be misleading. As John T. Noonan pointed out in his magisterial history of bribery, one country may have prosecuted more cases of corruption than another, yet actually have a much lower incidence of corruption, simply because the first country's will and capabilities to fight corruption are stronger.[6]

What about corruption in cities? Has it been growing worse? It has been argued that the substance and style of city management is changing in ways that promise better governance but also offer new temptations for corruption. A recent report from the Audit Commission of Great Britain summarizes these changes. "Many of the recent changes in local government," the Audit Commission asserts, "have been away from centralised controls and tight financial regimes and have increased the risks of fraud and corruption occurring."[7]

Administrative decentralization and municipal democratization are powerful trends. Over the past fifteen years, municipal governments have been asked to increase their responsibilities. At the same time, especially in developing countries, many municipalities have suffered an erosion in the real wages of officials. For all these reasons, concern with municipal corruption has grown. The Chilean policy analyst Claudio Orrego points out, "All the objectives that have been established for the reform of the municipal sector (increasing their legitimacy and democratization, increasing the efficiency and effectiveness of their services, and increasing citizen participation) can be summarized as part of this broader goal: *strengthening accountability.*"[8]

Noonan has mooted the hypothesis, without fully endorsing it, that a society tends to become *less* permissive of corruption as it becomes *more* permissive of sexual behavior.[9] Noonan notes that the unprecedented prosecution of corruption in the United States beginning in the 1970s took place after an unprecedented liberalization of sexual attitudes and behavior.[10]

As Noonan's notion illustrates, the question "why is corruption such a big issue now?" may lead down paths far removed from practical remedies. Whatever the reasons for today's greater concern over corruption, it is a change we should welcome. Simply put, corruption threatens economic and political development. We need to supplement today's concern about corruption with a deeper analysis of corrupt phenomena and more creative and practical thinking about how we can work together to deal with them.

WHY DO MANY EFFORTS TO COMBAT CORRUPTION FAIL?

Unfortunately, the history of anti-corruption campaigns around the world is not propitious. At the national and local levels, in ministries and in agencies such as the police, even highly publicized efforts to reduce corruption have tended to lurch, lapse, and, ultimately, disappoint.

A typical pattern looks something like this. A scandal occurs. For example, a municipal councilor may be found guilty of bribe-taking. Or the police may be found to be systematically involved in collusion with criminals. Public works programs may be found to contain inflated costs as the result of fraud and kickbacks.

Bidders on municipal projects may be discovered to have formed a collusive ring to restrict competition and inflate prices.

As the scandal erupts, the public is outraged. The press fulminates. Politicians express dismay and call for decisive action. An inquiry commission is formed. Six months later, the commission's recommendations emerge. They tend to include more layers of oversight, bigger budgets for investigation and enforcement, and a new code of conduct. But in the six months that have passed, the public's outrage has subsided, and so the press and politicians pay little attention to the recommendations. In fairness, this is partly because the recommendations tend to be expensive and to promise little real prevention.

It may be the case that, in the short run, heightened concern leads to reduced corruption in the agency concerned. But concern proves difficult to sustain and institutionalize. As a result, there are cycles of reform. After the crisis, there may be improvement. But in a while the corruption reemerges.[11]

In most countries, as sociologist Amitai Etzioni once pointed out,[12] there is no lobby to combat corruption. Unlike the circumstances associated with, say, sugar or soybeans or shoes, where a particular interest group is affected specifically by a change in policy, the costs of corruption are usually spread over a large number of people, usually taxpayers. Because the benefits of preventing corruption are also widespread, the logic of collective action predicts that an effective interest group will be hard to mobilize and sustain.

The recent formation of Transparency International (TI)[13] is an encouraging sign that this prediction may not hold forever. TI was founded in Berlin in 1993 and now has chapters in forty countries. It hopes to do for corruption what Amnesty International did for human rights. As we shall see, a key strategic concern for anti-corruption campaigns is how to mobilize and sustain popular participation in the fight against corruption.

Many anti-corruption efforts fail because they take an exclusively legalistic approach or rely on appeals to morality. Sometimes anti-corruption efforts are pursued only halfheartedly, because of the "seven excuses" of Box 2. Sometimes anti-corruption efforts themselves become corrupt efforts to vilify or imprison the opposition.

Fortunately, there are successful anti-corruption initiatives from which we can learn. They teach us that a key to success is to have a *strategy* for preventing corruption.

Box 2: Seven Invalid Excuses for Not Fighting Corruption

Excuse 1. "Corruption is everywhere. Japan has it, Holland has it, the United States has it. There's nothing you can do about something endemic." But consider health. Illness is everywhere, too. And yet no one concludes that efforts to prevent and treat illness should therefore be curtailed. Like illness, the levels and types of corruption vary greatly, and preventive and curative measures make a difference.

Excuse 2. "Corruption has always existed. Like sin, it's part of human nature. You can't do anything about it." Again, the observation is correct, the conclusion invalid. Because sin exists does not mean each of us sins to the same degree, and the same holds for corruption. We can constrain opportunities for corruption, even if the tendency is perennial.

Excuse 3. "The concept of corruption is vague and culturally determined. In some cultures the behavior that bothers you is not considered corrupt. Fighting corruption smacks of cultural imperialism." In fact, as John T. Noonan's monumental history shows, no culture condones bribery. Anthropological studies indicate that local people are perfectly capable of distinguishing a gift and a bribe, and they condemn bribery. The forms of corruption that this book considers are against the law in every city in the world.

Excuse 4. "Cleansing our society of corruption would require a wholesale change of attitudes and values. This can only take place after . . . [the polemicist's choice: a hundred years of education, a true revolution of the proletariat, a Christian or Muslim or other religious revival or state, and so forth]. Anything less will be futile." The record of moralization campaigns is not encouraging. More germane to city managers are two other points. First, engineering such massive social changes exceeds their scope of work. Second, in the meantime there are ways to close loopholes, create incentives and deterrents, augment accountability and competition, and improve the rules of the game.

Excuse 5. "In many countries corruption is not harmful at all. It is the grease for the wheels of the economy, and the glue of the political system." True, corrupt equilibrants do exist. But both theoretical models and empirical studies show that they are inferior to equilibrants with less corruption. Arguing that corrupt payments have a function in a given system does not at all argue for their aggregate desirability.

Excuse 6. "There's nothing that can be done if the man or woman at the top is corrupt, or if corruption is systematic." It is more propitious for anti-corruption efforts if leaders are clean and if corruption is episodic rather than routine. But success stories show that improved systems lead to fewer opportunities for everyone, even the political powers, to reap corrupt rents. Systematic corruption can be reduced.

Excuse 7. "Worrying about corruption is superfluous. With free markets and multiparty democracies, corruption will gradually disappear." Democracy and markets enhance competition and accountability, thereby reducing corruption. But during transitions, corruption may increase. In stable democracies, corruption is a chronic threat to the provision of many public goods and services, which are inherently the monopoly of the state (such as justice).

Formulating a Strategy

EXAMPLE OF A PREVENTIVE STRATEGY

Hong Kong's anti-corruption effort illustrates a major argument of this book: Fighting corruption should not be considered an end in itself but an orienting principle for reforming urban administration. In Hong Kong, a remarkable initiative to root out corruption, particularly in the police department, became a vehicle for the modernization of service delivery and the empowerment of citizens in local government.

The case also illustrates two other points. First, a sustainable strategy should address corrupt systems. Second, what might be called a culture of cynicism and impunity can be broken.

In the early 1970s Hong Kong police were deeply involved with drug traffickers, gambling dens, and prostitution rings, which paid the police to look the other way. The police department evolved its own syndicates to process corrupt receipts. For example, in the western district of Kowloon, one syndicate collected money from drug dens and vendors through middlemen and then on to middle-level officers. Higher-ranking officers would receive regular payments for keeping their eyes closed; and the syndicate worked out an elaborate scheme to distribute and manage its corrupt receipts, including accountants, payments to six banks, and in some cases the foreign remission of funds. Lower-ranking officers also participated in "fixing" traffic violations for immediate bribes. Police officers also extorted money from tea shops and street vendors. Corruption plagued the internal merit systems, and the police force's internal Anti-Corruption Office was itself corrupted.

The new governor commissioned a major review, which uncovered shocking evidence of such institutional sickness. The commission's description is worth quoting at length, because it exemplifies an often-overlooked phenomenon of broader relevance: systematic corruption.

> *The worst forms are what are described . . . as "syndicated" corruption, that is to say a whole group of officers involved in the collection and distribution of money. . . . Frequently the "collection" is far more than corruption in the true sense. It is plain extortion accompanied by the veiled threats of violence at the hands of triad gangsters. . . .*
>
> *Many police officers, so it is said, have simply lost heart in their endeavor to deal with a number of "social" offenses and have joined the ranks of those who "squeeze" the operators rather than take them to court. . . .*
>
> *It is said that Police corruption is, for the most part, "syndicated" and that corruption on an individual basis is frowned upon by the organizers of these "syndicates"—indeed anyone operating on his own is liable to be "fixed." The organizers are good psychologists. New arrivals in the Force are tested to see how strong is their sense of duty. The testing may take various forms—sums of money placed on their desks, etc. If an officer fails to report the first overture*

of this sort he is really "hooked" for the rest of his service, and is afraid to report any corrupt activities which may thereafter come to his notice. . . .

[T]here is a saying in Hong Kong:

1. *"Get on the bus," i.e., if you wish to accept corruption, join us;*
2. *"Run alongside the bus," i.e., if you do not wish to accept corruption, it matters not, but do not interfere;*
3. *"Never stand in front of the bus," i.e., if you try to report corruption, the "bus" will knock you down and you will be injured or even killed or your business will be ruined. We will get you somehow.*

The reaction of honest young police officers hearing this kind of talk may well be imagined. They either join the "bus" or mind their own business.[1]

Police corruption was creating a climate of distrust in the entire government, at a time when Hong Kong was experiencing pressures from a "new class" of young professionals for a more democratic and participatory government. Moreover, a corrupted police force facilitated the spread of corruption in other government agencies. Hong Kong's international reputation was suffering. One study showed that 70 percent of news stories about Hong Kong in the British press had to do with corrupt practices.[2] With corruption burgeoning, it was feared that investment and trade might increasingly turn elsewhere.

Corruption was growing, but it was certainly not new. Nor was it novel to be concerned about it. There had been many previous attempts to deal with police corruption, each of which had emphasized what might be called "the usual solutions"—stronger laws, more resources and power to the Anti-Corruption Office within the police department, and an emphasis on investigation. For example, over time authorities were permitted to examine the bank accounts of government employees, first when a specific corrupt act was investigated, later when an official's "standard of living" and "control of pecuniary resources" were deemed excessive. The next step was to allow such officials to be dismissed on the basis of "unexplained enrichment." When this did not work, the next step shifted the burden of proof for such cases: Those accused would have to demonstrate their innocence. The police's Anti-Corruption Office gained new powers to gather information and long-term intelligence, to investigate alleged acts of corruption, and to delve into the lifestyles of officials.

Despite it all, corruption continued. When corruption is systematic, often the usual solutions won't work. Indeed, the usual reflex toward more rules and further layers of oversight may be counterproductive even in the cities of the richest countries of the world, as Frank Anechiarico and James B. Jacobs have argued about New York.[3]

Fortunately, Hong Kong's new governor, Murray MacLehose, did not follow the usual lines of attack. Instead, he adopted a bold new strategy. He set up a new Independent Commission against Corruption (ICAC), which reported directly to him, and abolished the police Anti-Corruption Office. The ICAC did have powerful investigatory capabilities, but from the beginning it emphasized *prevention and citizen participation.*

The ICAC had three components:

1. Operations Department, which was in charge of investigations

2. Corruption Prevention Department (CPD), which evaluated where various agencies were vulnerable to corruption and helped the agencies take remedial measures
3. Community Relations Department (CRD), which involved the people of Hong Kong in the fight against corruption

The ICAC's strategy recognized the need to rupture the culture of corruption. As other success stories also teach, an important step in fighting systematic corruption is to "fry big fish," that is, to prosecute and punish high-level perpetrators. Hong Kong successfully extradited a former chief superintendent, who had escaped to England and was enjoying there an ill-gotten fortune. The extradition signaled that the rules of the game had changed, and that all the good words about preventing corruption would be backed by action.

The Corruption Prevention Department recruited sixty-five specialists, including management experts, systems analysts, computer experts, accountants, lawyers, engineers, and architects. In the words of one CPD official, it was

> *responsible for taking a good, hard look at practices and procedures within the Government and public utilities. We do this through careful examination and analysis of systems, methods, work approach, and policies. The object is to eliminate, and simplify wherever possible or desirable, unenforceable laws, cumbersome procedures, [and] vague and ineffectual practices conducive to corruption.*

The CPD established two divisions. A "people" division dealt with services and personnel functions; and a "property" division worked with contracts, buildings, and land. The ICAC kept a low profile and established a "you-take-the-credit" relationship with the various government agencies. If agencies were unwilling to analyze their situations with the ICAC's help or if after such analysis needed changes were not made, the implicit threat was the governor's wrath, publicity, and strong action. But the threat did not need to be carried out. Together, the CPD and government agencies identified areas of excessive or unregulated discretion, poor control systems, and unenforceable rules and regulations. The ICAC's 1975 annual report called the CPD "an entirely new concept in public administration," and a measure of pride is understandable. The results went beyond the control of corruption. The government now had a new tool to reform the delivery of public services.

The ICAC was also a strategic device to mobilize citizen participation and support. This was accomplished in two ways.

First, five citizen advisory committees were set up to guide and monitor the ICAC. They included government critics, and their scope ranged from overall policy through the functions of the ICAC to a "complaints committee." The idea of a citizen oversight board has, we believe, wide relevance for ensuring the transparency of government agencies, especially those with powers as great as the ICAC's.

Second, the ICAC's Community Relations Department was another strategic innovation. The CRD set up local offices to gather information about corruption from civil society as well as to engage in grassroots educational activities about corruption's evils. The CRD also created school programs, publicity campaigns, filmstrips, TV dramas, a radio call-in show, special pamphlets, and exhibitions.

The results were remarkable. Systematic corruption in the police force was broken. Moreover, corruption throughout Hong

Box 3: Key Features of the Hong Kong Strategy

1. When confronted with systematic corruption, understand that the usual law enforcement approaches are insufficient. Even Draconian powers of investigation fail when the investigatory mechanism is corrupted.
2. Create a new, independent anti-corruption agency with carefully selected, talented staff with intrepid leadership and powerful internal controls. Create five citizen oversight boards to guide and monitor the agency. Both steps provide credibility.
3. Break the culture of cynicism and compliance by "frying big fish."
4. Then emphasize prevention. Systematically analyze government functions. Move to reduce monopoly power, clarify and streamline discretion, and promote accountability. Work with government agencies, not against them. At the same time as this fights corruption, it enables radical changes in the delivery of public services.
5. Mobilize citizens in the fight against corruption by creating many new avenues to receive information from them about corruption and to educate them about its harms. At the same time as this battles corruption, it enables radical changes in citizens' participation and support.
6. In sum, understand that systematic corruption requires a systematic approach and radical changes. Also, fighting corruption can be a lever for a general reform of local government.

Kong was reduced. The ICAC prosecuted officials from the departments of Fire, Housing, Immigration, Labor, Marine, Medical and Health, New Territories Administration, Post Office, Prisons, Public Works, Transport, and Urban Services. The ICAC also investigated and prosecuted corruption within the private sector. The ICAC worked proactively with the leaders and managers of many government departments. Within seven years, the Corruption Prevention Department had carried out almost 500 studies on various policies and practices in government agencies. It followed up many of these with full-scale monitoring reports on how well the recommendations were being implemented. In those first seven years, its seminars on corruption prevention were attended by more than 10,000 officials.

Perhaps the ICAC's most important benefits underscore a theme of this book: Preventing corruption can be the point of leverage for reinventing city government. In Hong Kong, thanks to initiatives spearheaded by the ICAC, city services became more efficient, and the people of Hong Kong had new ways to participate in and influence their government.

Box 3 summarizes some of the key features of Hong Kong's successful strategy against corruption.[4]

HOW TO FORMULATE A STRATEGY

The need for a *strategy* may sound obvious, but anti-corruption campaigns often lack just that. Corruption should not be conceived as a mere irregularity or the act of a scoundrel. The secret of successful reform is changing policies and systems, rather than hunting for isolated culprits, adding new laws and regulations, or calling for a moral renovation. Where there is the combination of monopoly plus official discretion minus accountability, we will tend to find corruption. When public officials are paid meager salaries and offered no rewards or incentives for exceptional performance, and when penalties against the corrupt are rare and mild, we can expect corruption to flourish. Successful reforms address these systemic problems.

To some people, however, there is no reason even to talk about a campaign against corruption or a new strategy. The only thing needed is for the government to do what it should be doing. A vice president of a major international agency recently wrote the senior author to this effect. The problem with African governments, he said, wasn't figuring out what to do about corruption. It was for governments to do what they already promised to be doing but weren't.

This reaction contains an element of truth, and this element has parallels in many areas of life. A company would be more profitable if only everyone in the company more fully lived up to her or his responsibilities. We would all be better people if only we reminded ourselves of our deepest precepts and did a better job of living up to them.

But in another sense the vice president's reaction begs the interesting questions. Why *don't* we live up to our best? Are there practical strategies of self-control that might help us do better? Shelves of self-help books try to provide tips. Regarding companies, a vast literature deals with how business leaders can induce employees to live up to their responsibilities. The fact that so many books exist implies that the answers are not obvious.

So it is for a campaign against corruption. If one could simply say "don't bribe and don't take bribes" and be heeded, that would be the end of bribery. But it's not that simple. It is costly to monitor and costly to punish, so that finding out whether one is heeded and punishing those who don't heed isn't free and easy.

One must create a climate, an information structure, and a set of incentives so that government employees and private citizens engage in the optimal amounts of corruption of various kinds. This requires understanding what induces various kinds of corruption and how they cause social harm (and occasionally some social benefits) and what the benefits *and the costs* are of various anti-corruption measures. Then it requires an implementation plan for moving from where we are to where we hope to be, taking account of the costs of doing so.

What is a *strategy* against corruption? The beginning of the answer is that a strategy focuses on corrupt systems, not (just) corrupt individuals. In other words, instead of thinking about corruption in terms of an immoral individual breaking the law and violating a trust (which are true), one thinks about systems that are more and less susceptible to various illicit activities.

Much can be said about the kinds of governments, and more generally the kinds of institutions be they public, private, or non-profit, that are susceptible to corruption. Corruption tends to be reduced by the separation of powers; checks and balances; transparency; a good system of justice; and clearly defined roles, responsibilities, rules, and limits. Corruption tends not to thrive where there is a democratic culture, competition, and good systems of control, and where people (employees, clients, overseers) have rights to information and rights of redress. Corruption loves multiple and complex regulations with ample and uncheckable official discretion.

Notice that most of these ideas apply to businesses as well as governments. So does a metaphorical formula we find useful:

$$\mathbf{C} = \mathbf{M} + \mathbf{D} - \mathbf{A}$$

Corruption (C) equals monopoly power (M) plus discretion by officials (*D*) minus accountability (*A*).[5] If someone has monopoly power over a good or service and has the discretion to decide whether someone gets that good or service or how much a person receives, and there is no accountability whereby others can see what that person is deciding, then we will tend to find corruption. This is true whether we are in the public sector or the private, whether we are in a poor country or a rich one, whether we are in Beira or Berlin or Beirut.

A strategy against corruption, therefore, should not begin or end with fulmination about ethics or the need for a new set of attitudes. Instead, it should cold-bloodedly look for ways to reduce monopoly power, limit and clarify discretion, and increase transparency, all the while taking account of the costs, both direct and indirect, of these ways.

There is another crucial point in designing an anti-corruption strategy: Corruption is a crime of calculation, not of passion. People will tend to engage in corruption when the risks are low, the penalties mild, and the rewards great. This insight overlaps the formula just mentioned, because the rewards will be the greater as monopoly power increases. But it adds the idea that incentives at the margin are what determine the calculations of corrupt and potentially corrupt officials and citizens. Change information and incentives, and you change corruption.

Having a strategy also means that we should usually not attack all forms of corruption at once. We must distinguish various types of corruption and recognize that they are not all equally harmful, even if we do not say so in public. For example, systematic corruption in the police is usually more pernicious than corruption in the Driver's License Department. In general, inspectors of all varieties must be cleaner than service providers must be. Having a strategy means developing a clear idea of ends and means in the short, medium, and long terms. To be credible, an anti-corruption campaign needs an early success. But it also requires a five-year plan with phased, realistic goals.

We can usefully separate what might be called *economic* issues from the *implementation* issues in preventing corruption. As we will see below, economic models prove useful in addressing such questions as:

1. What are the costs (and the possible benefits) of various forms of illicit behavior?
2. For each kind or area of corruption, what kinds of preventive measures might reduce corruption?
3. What are the benefits in terms of reduced corruption and perhaps enhanced efficiency of the preventive measures? What are the costs of these measures?
4. What are the interactions among various anti-corruption measures, both positive and negative?
5. Given the answers to the above, what sequence of measures should be adopted at what levels?

What might be called the implementation issues go further. For example, how can allies be mobilized and potential enemies neutralized or coopted? How will the choice of measures in this domain help or hinder the policy maker's (or government's) ability to move in other important domains? How can the officials implementing the policies gain ownership over what is done? How can the officials' incentives be altered to improve the chances that what is designed gets implemented?

Of course, economic issues and implementation overlap. Fighting corruption should not be viewed as an end in itself, for two reasons. At some point the economic costs of reducing corruption outweigh the benefits of further reductions. But a strategic point for municipal reformers cuts in the opposite direction. Done correctly, a strategy for preventing corruption can be the lever for a city's financial recovery, the reform of service delivery, and the involvement of citizens. Beyond the reduction in malfeasance lies the prospect of reinventing local government.

CHAPTER 3

Corruption as a System

AN ECONOMIC APPROACH TO CORRUPTION

How might one develop a strategy for preventing corruption in a specific setting? In this book we stress several steps:

1. understanding corrupt systems, which requires analytical tools (this chapter);
2. diagnosing how specific corrupt systems now work in a particular context (Chapter 4);
3. overcoming political and bureaucratic resistance, and garnering support (Chapters 4 and 5); and
4. crafting a sequenced plan of action to heal corrupted systems, rupture a culture of cynicism, build political momentum, and transform city government (Chapter 5).

The present section emphasizes an economic approach to corruption. Corruption is a crime of economic calculation. If the probability of being caught is small and the penalty is mild and the pay-off is large relative to the positive incentives facing the government official, then we will tend to find corruption. Fortunately, economic analysis suggests that it is possible to locate areas within an organization where corruption is most likely. As mentioned in the previous chapter, a heuristic formula holds: Corruption equals monopoly plus discretion of officials minus accountability.

When we think of prevention, we should think of changes in the incentives facing officials, including increasing penalties, raising the probability of being caught, and linking pay to performance. We should seek to reduce monopoly, clarify discretion, and enhance accountability.

This section elaborates on these principles and derives a framework for policy analysis. But first, to demonstrate the relevance of what may appear to be theoretical abstractions, Mayor MacLean-Abaroa describes how he used them to guide his reformation of La Paz's municipal administration.

Wherever I found problems in service delivery or the prompt completion of public works or the collection of revenues, they happened not just to be associated with inefficient organization but almost always with corruption. The more I learned about municipal performance, the more I tripped over suspect behavior. So I turned around and started using the formula of corruption $C = M + D - A$ *as the organizing principle for my attempt to reinvent city government in La Paz. (In Spanish there is no word for "accountability," so we use "transparency" and the formula is* $C = M + D - T$*.)*

I came to realize that the introduction of competition, the reduction of bureaucratic discretion and leeway, and the increase of accountability were the keys to solving my institutional bottlenecks and roadblocks. In fact, I have come to believe that in La Paz, as perhaps in other municipalities, years and decades of predatory behavior by public institutions have developed systematic or intrinsic corruption. In a Darwinian way, these sick institutions seem to have evolved into complex and sophisticated corruption machines, with a shape, size, and modus operandi *and also the statutory legitimacy "fit" for corruption.*

I could give many examples. Let me just describe one.

Construction permits were a great source of corruption and frustration. According to existing city legislation, ***all*** *new construction work in the city had to be approved by the Urban Development Department of the municipality. Not only that, any modification in existing construction, such as remodeling or just putting in a new door outside or* ***inside*** *any building, also had to be authorized. Needless to say, waiting to receive all these authorizations could amount to years—unless you paid a bribe.*

I learned of the corruption and applied the formula. This led, first, to a reconsideration of which permits were necessary and to a redesign of the processes for granting permits. We deregulated. For the regulations that stayed, we simplified the procedures and publicized them, so that citizens could not be tricked into thinking that a regulation said something it didn't or involved steps it didn't.

We also began to break the monopoly of granting permits, which in turn led me to solve a structural problem. In fact, even if corruption had not existed, the formula's anticorruption "medicine" turned out in many areas of city government to be perfect for avoiding costly inefficiency and delays as well as an expensive burden on municipal resources.

There are certain professions with a surplus of supply in Bolivia, and one of them is architecture. So I decided to propose that the professional association of architects make it possible for members to become certified by the city, so they could grant the construction permits on behalf of the city, complying with city norms and regulations, and for a fee which the market would set. The architects in turn would have to pass an exam demonstrating knowledge of the city's regulatory norms, called USPA, and deposit a bond that the city would collect if they failed to perform their duty professionally and honestly. The architects' association had to agree to help implement, monitor, and if need be sanction.

We did not get this step implemented until 1996, after I was reelected. We added more than a hundred private architects to cope with the huge demand for permits, cutting waiting time dramatically. Certified architects just filled in a form with all the necessary information and issued a signed, sealed, and numbered construction permit. Then a few, well-paid officials of the Urban Development Department would conduct a sample test of some of the permits and go through a complete checkup. If irregularities surfaced, the city could take action along with the architects' association, which could also advocate on behalf of its members should officials extort them with improper allegations. The illegal market for corruption, where delays and monopoly raised the price, was thereby subverted.

This is one example of a broad principle. I used the formula $C = M + D - A$ *as the marco ordenador [guiding principle] of my terms as mayor.*

CORRUPTION AS A CRIME OF CALCULATION

The formula to which MacLean-Abaroa refers begins with an observation in the spirit of economics. It is true that different individuals react differently to the temptations of corruption, and many public and private officials refrain from corruption even when the temptations are great. But it is crucial for fighting corruption to recognize that as temptations rise so do levels of corruption.

What induces temptation? The Nicaraguan accountant Francisco Ramírez Torres discusses at length such factors as family, school, attitudes toward work, the business or ministry, the nation, and the international situation. At the level of the individual, he cites as causes of corruption excessive consumption of alcohol, extramarital activities, speculative losses, gambling, "causes related to vanity," administrative disorganization, "the thirst for illicit enrichment," and eight others.[1] Let us oversimplify the complex reality Ramírez Torres describes.

As a first approximation, officials will be tempted to engage in corruption when the size of their corrupt gain is greater than the penalty if caught times the probability of being caught. The penalty includes the wage and other incentives they must sacrifice if they lose their jobs, as well as the severity of the punishment.

When will the size of the corrupt gain be large? Officials will have the opportunity to garner corrupt benefits as a function of their degree of monopoly over a service or activity, their discretion in deciding who should get how much, and the degree to which their activities are accountable.

How, then, should we try to control corruption? One approach is to lessen monopoly, clarify and limit discretion, and enhance accountability.

Of course reducing corruption is not our only concern. We might spend so much money attacking corruption, or generate so much red tape and bureaucracy, that the costs and losses in efficiency would outweigh the benefits of lower corruption.

It may be worthwhile at this point to use an economic metaphor. Suppose you are the principal and we are your agents. The principal may be the mayor of a city, the head of a department, or the manager of a benefits program. Let us suppose that you are not corrupt and that your objectives coincide with the public's interest. But as your agents, we are tempted by corruption. You wish to induce us to undertake productive activities and to deter our corrupt activities. Therefore, you consider reducing our (or our agency's) monopoly powers, clarifying and sometimes circumscribing our discretion over who receives how much service for what price, and enhancing accountability. You want to increase our incentives to undertake socially productive activities and raise the effective penalties for corruption.

But each of these possible initiatives may be costly, in several dimensions. They may cost money. They may carry opportunity costs. They may create externalities. Your economic problem is therefore much more complicated than "fighting corruption." Ideally, you would balance the benefits of your efforts (in terms of improved productivity and reduced costs of corruption, which you would need to estimate) and their costs.

A FRAMEWORK FOR POLICY ANALYSIS

From these considerations, one can derive a "framework for policy analysis" (see Box 4). It is not a recipe but a device for stimulating the creative and analytical abilities of those interested in controlling corruption.

According to this framework, the principal may select agents, alter their incentives, collect information in order to raise the probabilities of detecting and punishing corruption, change the relationship between agents and clients, and raise the moral costs of corruption. Working through this framework with top officials, businesses, and citizens has proved useful in many countries in helping them think through alternatives.

Box 4: Preventing Corruption: A Framework for Policy Analysis

A. Select agents.
   1. Screen out the dishonest (using past records, tests, and predictors of honesty).
   2. Beef up recruitment by merit and circumvent nepotism.
   3. Exploit outside "guarantees" of honesty (use networks for finding dependable agents and making sure they stay that way).

B. Set agents' rewards and penalties.
   1. Change rewards.
      a. Raise salaries to reduce the need for corrupt income.
      b. Reward specific actions and agents that reduce corruption.
      c. Improve career paths so that promotions depend on performance.
      d. Use contingent contracts to reward agents on the basis of eventual success (for example, forfeitable nonvested pensions or performance bonds).
      e. Link nonmonetary rewards to performance (training, transfers, perks, travel, publicity, or praise)
   2. Penalize corrupt behavior.
      a. Raise the severity of formal penalties.
      b. Increase the principal's authority to punish.
      c. Calibrate penalties in terms of deterrent effects and breaking the culture of corruption.
      d. Use a range of penalties (training; transfers; publicity; blackballing; and loss of professional standing, perks, and travel privileges).

C. Obtain information about efforts and results.
   1. Improve auditing and management information systems.
      a. Gather evidence about possible corruption (using red flags, statistical analysis, random samples of work, and inspections).

b. Carry out "vulnerability assessments"—see Box 11.

2. Strengthen information agents.
   a. Beef up specialized staff (auditors, computer specialists, investigators, supervisors, and internal security).
   b. Create a climate in which agents (for example, whistle-blowers) will report improper activities.
   c. Create new units (ombudsmen, special investigatory committees, anti-corruption agencies, or inquiry commissions).
3. Collect information from third parties (media and banks).
4. Collect information from clients and the public (including professional associations).
5. Change the burden of proof, so that the potentially corrupt (for example, public servants with great wealth) have to demonstrate their innocence.

D. Restructure the principal-agent-client relationship to weaken monopoly power, circumscribe discretion, and enhance accountability.

1. Induce competition in the provision of the good or service (through privatization, public-private competition, and competition among public agents).
2. Limit agents' discretion.
   a. Define objectives, rules, and procedures more clearly and publicize them.
   b. Have agents work in teams and subject them to hierarchical review.
   c. Divide large decisions into separable tasks.
   d. Clarify and circumscribe agents' influence over key decisions (change decision rules, change decision makers, and alter incentives).
3. Rotate agents functionally and geographically.
4. Change the organization's mission, product, or technology to render it less susceptible to corruption.

5. Organize client groups to render them less susceptible to some forms of corruption, to promote information flows, and to create an anti-corruption lobby.

E. Raise the "moral costs" of corruption.

1. Use training, educational programs, and personal example.
2. Promulgate a code of ethics (for civil service, profession, or agency).
3. Change the corporate culture.

The following are a few notes for municipal leaders to consider regarding several of the framework's most important categories:

Selecting agents. The agents of course include municipal officials, but notice that the agents that carry out municipal works need not be municipal employees. Many cities have taken on too many tasks and have become *de facto* monopolists. If instead services can be contracted out to competitive markets and performance can be carefully assessed (including by citizens—see "Enhance accountability and transparency" later in this chapter), then efficiency will be enhanced and corruption will be reduced. As with all levels of government, one of the most important anti-corruption measures can be the outsourcing of tasks and functions to private agents.

Improve the positive incentives facing municipal officials. In many cities, pay levels have fallen so low that officials literally cannot feed their families without moonlighting or accepting side payments. Even more important is to strengthen the linkages between pay and performance, and promotion and performance, which in many cities have badly eroded.

Increase the effective penalties for corruption. Because of weak or corrupt investigatory, prosecutory, and judicial systems, accusations of corruption seldom stick. If they do, the penalties are often minimal in practice (for example, the official is fired). As a result, the expected penalty for corruption (the chance of being caught and convicted times penalty if convicted) has no power to deter. A key step is to strengthen the capacity and improve the incentives of the police, prosecutors, and judges. But of course city governments usually do not control these agencies. Nonetheless, municipal leaders can be creative in devising disincentives, such as firing or suspending employees, using the press to create publicity, inviting the denunciation of corrupt officials by professional groups, transferring people to less desirable jobs, and so forth.

Limit monopoly. Promote competition in the public and private sectors. Avoid monopoly-granting regulations when possible.

Clarify official discretion. Simplify rules and regulations. Create "bright lines" that circumscribe duties and discretion. Help citizens learn how public systems are supposed to work (through brochures and manuals, help desks, laws and rules in ordinary language, publicity campaigns, using citizens as service providers, and so on). Improve citizens' oversight of what the city government is doing.

Enhance accountability and transparency. Clear standards of conduct and rules of the game make accountability easier. So does openness in bidding, grant-giving, and aid projects. Accountability depends on the capabilities of internal auditors, accountants, ombudsmen, inspectors, specialized elements of the police, and specialized prosecutors. But accountability also should involve citizens, unions, nongovernment organizations (NGOs), the media, and business in a variety of ways, including citizen oversight boards, hotlines, external audits, inquiry commissions, and so forth. City governments can help external actors by generating and disseminating more information about public service effectiveness. Finally, cities should encourage the private sector to police its own participation in corrupt schemes of procurement, contracting, regulating, and so forth.

APPLYING THE FRAMEWORK TO HONG KONG

Many of these headings are useful in summarizing the strategy of Hong Kong's Independent Commission against Corruption. It is not of course that Jack Cater and his staff had Box 4 explicitly in

Box 5: The Framework for Policy Analysis Applied to Hong Kong

A. Select agents.

1. Screen out the dishonest (using past records, tests, and predictors of honesty). Only some of the staff of the old Anti-Corruption Office of the police were appointed to the ICAC, after much screening.
2. Beef up recruitment by merit and circumvent nepotism. Strong use of merit principle to recruit accountants, auditors, systems analysts, and other specialists.
3. Exploit outside "guarantees" of honesty. As a colony, Hong Kong could "import" senior police officers.

B. Set agents' rewards and penalties.

1. Change rewards.
   a. Raise salaries to reduce the need for corrupt income. A special 10 percent pay allowance was added for ICAC staff.
   b. Reward specific actions and agents that reduce corruption.
   c. Improve career paths so that promotions depend on performance. Civil service rules were not in force in the ICAC, and promotion could be rapid.
   d. Use contingent contracts to reward agents on the basis of eventual success (for example, forfeitable nonvested pensions or performance bonds). Most ICAC staff were on two-and-one-half–year contracts and were carefully evaluated before being renewed.
   e. Link nonmonetary rewards to performance (training, transfers, perks, travel, publicity, or praise)
2. Penalize corrupt behavior.
   a. Raise the severity of formal penalties. The Hong Kong government went after some "big fish" early, and their apprehension and punishment were widely publicized.

b. Increase the principal's authority to punish. The ICAC had the power to dismiss any employee at any time.

c. Calibrate penalties in terms of deterrent effects and breaking the culture of corruption.

d. Use a range of penalties (training; transfers; publicity; blackballing; and loss of professional standing, perks, and travel privileges).

C. Obtain information about efforts and results. This was perhaps the greatest source of the ICAC's success.

1. Improve auditing and management information systems.

a. Gather evidence about possible corruption (using red flags, statistical analysis, random samples of work, and inspections). The ICAC used many of these techniques to gauge the extent of corruption. Undercover agents were also used.

b. Carry out "vulnerability assessments." The ICAC analyzed many public agencies, working in concert with them rather than with a hostile attitude. Leaders of those agencies were allowed to take credit for reforms that prevented corruption and enhanced efficiencies, with the ICAC acting almost as management consultants.

2. Strengthen information agents.

a. Beef up specialized staff (auditors, computer specialists, investigators, supervisors, and internal security). The ICAC emphasized prevention and recruited a large number of such specialists for the Corruption Prevention Department.

b. Create a climate in which agents (for example, whistleblowers) will report improper activities. Many opportunities were open, ranging from anonymous complaints to local offices where citizens could present their grievances. The ICAC had a twenty-four-hour hotline for complaints.

c. Create new units (ombudsmen, special investigatory committees, anti-corruption agencies, or inquiry commissions). The Community Relations Department was designed in part to garner information from the public. The ICAC's citizens' oversight boards helped provide information as well as credible insurance that the ICAC's many powers would not be abused.

3. Collect information from third parties (media and banks). The ICAC applied strong laws that enabled it to investigate the possibly ill-gotten wealth of public employees, including bank accounts.
4. Collect information from clients and the public (including professional associations). The Community Relations Department obtained much information from citizens about corruption and inefficiency. The oversight boards included professionals in areas relevant to the ICAC's work.
5. Change the burden of proof, so that the potentially corrupt (for example, public servants with great wealth) have to demonstrate their innocence. This is exactly what the ICAC implemented.

D. Restructure the principal-agent-client relationship to weaken monopoly power, circumscribe discretion, and enhance accountability.

1. Induce competition in the provision of the good or service (through privatization, public-private competition, or competition among public agents).
2. Limit agents' discretion.
   a. Define objectives, rules, and procedures more clearly and publicize them.
   b. Have agents work in teams and subject them to hierarchical review.
   c. Divide large decisions into separable tasks.

d. Clarify and circumscribe agents' influence over key decisions (change decision rules, change decision makers, or alter incentives). The ICAC established a strong system of internal controls, which among other things limited discretion and enhanced accountability.

3. Rotate agents functionally and geographically.
4. Change the organization's mission, product, or technology to render it less susceptible to corruption. The ICAC became much more than an investigatory agency. It emphasized prevention and community relations as the keys to the long-term strategy.
5. Organize client groups to render them less susceptible to some forms of corruption, to promote information flows, and to create an anti-corruption lobby. The Community Relations Department set up local community offices, which helped citizens resist corruption, report it, and lobby against it.

E. Raise the "moral costs" of corruption.

1. Use training, educational programs, and personal example. The Community Relations Department engaged in many programs of civic education, ranging from schools to the media.
2. Promulgate a code of ethics (for civil service, profession, or agency). The ICAC established a strong code of conduct.
3. Change the corporate culture. The ICAC credibly established a "cleaner than clean" ethic and, through the transparency provided by its citizen oversight board, created structures to ensure it stayed that way.

mind, but rather that their own analysis of the problems of corruption also emphasized the importance of systematic reforms. Consider, for example, Box 5. It shows how the headings of Box 4 capture many of the key initiatives of the ICAC.

THE EXAMPLE OF PROCUREMENT

Procurement provides another example of the usefulness of Box 4. This is probably the area of municipal government where the greatest amount of corruption occurs, in terms of money values. Procurement corruption comes in a wide variety of forms. Among the principal types are:

1. collusion among bidders, leading to higher prices for the city which may or may not be shared with corrupt officials;
2. kickbacks by firms to city officials in order to "fix" procurement competition; and
3. bribes to city officials who regulate the winning contractor's behavior. The existence of this sort of corruption may encourage abnormally low bids, which being below estimated costs win the contract but then are "rectified" in the corrupt contractor's calculation by the subsequent cost overruns and lucrative changes in contract specifications that the bribe-taking regulator permits.

Box 6 shows how the framework for policy analysis leads to useful suggestions for each of these three problems.

The Appendix expounds this box in detail, exploring the complications of and the opportunities for reducing corruption through better and more efficient procurement systems.

Box 6: The Framework for Policy Analysis Applied to Deterring Collusion in Procurement

A. Select bidders.
   1. Screen for honesty (surveillance showing no collusion; background checks on contractors; and performance on past contracts).
   2. Exploit outside guarantees of honest bids and faithful performance.
   3. Allow only one firm to bid and negotiate ruthlessly.

B. Change the rewards and penalties facing bidders.
   1. Shift rewards to favor honest bids (later payment depending on costs and quality; incentive contracts).
   2. Change penalties to make collusion less attractive (disqualify colluding firms; employ criminal sanctions; or use publicity to damage company name).

C. Use informational strategies to raise the likelihood that collusion is detected and punished.
   1. Use systems for detecting collusion.
   2. Strengthen agents for gathering information (undercover work, surveillance, market prices, and cost estimation).
   3. Involve third parties to obtain credible information (industry newsletters and consultants, independent cost estimates, or auditors).
   4. Use bidders as sources of information (disaffected employees, losing bidders, those who choose not to bid).

D. Restructure the procurer-bidder relationship.
   1. Foment competition among bidders (new firms, wider publicity, lower barrier to entry, risk-sharing contracts, and requirements to share contract information).
   2. Reduce the discretion of your own agents (rules about change orders, follow-ons, "emergencies," sealed bids, decision rules for deciding among bidders, and hierarchical review of decisions).

3. Rotate your own agents.
4. Redefine the organization's "product" (more standardized goods with market prices; choosing inputs, outputs, and modes of payment with an eye to corruptibility; and vertical integration—make it rather than buy it).

E. Change attitudes about collusion.
1. Disassociate collusion from acceptable practices (such as export cartels) and goals (such as maximizing foreign exchange earnings).
2. Educate contractors about how competitive bidding works elsewhere.
3. Promote the bidders' identification with the social or public purpose of the contract.

Assessing Corruption

Economic analysis can be helpful in diagnosing where corruption might tend to occur and how the tendency might be attenuated. In a particular setting, how might one utilize the framework for policy analysis that we have just reviewed?

PARTICIPATORY DIAGNOSIS

In our experience, the very people who work in systematically corrupt institutions will help to analyze where and how that corruption occurs. This may be surprising, but it is often true—as long as the focus is on corrupt systems and not particular individuals. In workshops on corruption, which the senior author has facilitated in a dozen countries, after some time people turn out to be remarkably forthcoming about the corruption that exists, how it works, and how it might be prevented—even when their analyses belie an intimate knowledge that can only be incriminating.

In systematically corrupt settings, many politicians and officials hold complicated, mixed feelings about corruption. They may sincerely loathe it and wish to eradicate it, while at the same time participating in it or allowing it to occur. Psychologists and police apparently encounter similar phenomena. How might these mixed feelings be used to diagnose corrupt systems?

What Participatory Diagnosis Is

The simple answer is to enable people to discuss such systems analytically and without fear of reprisal. We sometimes use the metaphor of a *therapeutic approach to a sick institution.* Since corruption is a concept freighted with emotion and shame and defensiveness, the first task is to demystify corruption. In our workshops on corruption, we begin by having participants analyze a case study of a successful anti-corruption campaign in another country. Participants see that the problems can be analyzed coolly and dealt with effectively. Even though the other country's setting is inevitably different from their country's, the mere fact that both successful analysis and successful action occurred stills their skepticism and stimulates their creativity.

Then **analytical frameworks** are supplied that help participants realize that corruption is not (just or primarily) a problem of evil people but of corrupt systems. The corruption formula—corruption equals monopoly plus discretion minus accountability—is presented. To members of corrupt organizations, this insight often proves therapeutic.

As in good therapy, the participants then move to **self-diagnosis and self-prescription**. The results can be remarkable. Corrupt systems are diagnosed, and a useful start is made as to how they might be rectified. Out of such participatory diagnoses two things can emerge: a deeper, shared understanding of corrupt systems and a plan of action for reforming them.

How Participatory Diagnosis Might Be Carried Out

Such workshops can and perhaps should occur at many levels of a municipality, but it is important that the first one involve the highest levels. Ideally, the mayor or president of the city council convenes the workshop. In some cases the exercise is kept internal to the municipal government; in some cases outsiders are included. Directors, managers, councilors, police officials, heads of labor unions, heads of business groups, civic associations, and even heads of religious organizations may participate. The ideal number of participants is twenty to twenty-five. The ideal format is one to two days, in the mode of a retreat. Another possibility is two hours a day for five days.

The first session analyzes a case of a successful anti-corruption effort in another country. The case is presented in two parts. First are the problems, conveyed via slides. Then participants split into subgroups of about eight people. Each subgroup is asked to describe the types of corruption in the case, discuss which type is most serious and which least, list alternative anti-corruption measures and their pros and cons, and make a tentative recommendation. The subgroups then present summaries of their deliberations to a plenary session. After discussion, the second part of the case is presented: what the country or city in question actually did, and the results. Participants then discuss what happened and why. Even though the context inevitably differs from their own, they are stimulated by the careful analysis and by the fact that reforms worked.

Then after a break, there is a lecture on the economics of corruption, focusing on motive and opportunity, and on the equation $C = M + D - A$. Questions and discussion are encouraged. The framework for policy analysis in Box 4 is presented and reviewed.

Then the group analyzes a second case study, again of a success story. This case requires them to provide not only for what might be called an economic analysis of corruption and how to fight it, but for a political and bureaucratic strategy. Three lessons emerge from the case. First, in order to break the culture of corruption and cynicism, "big fish" must be fried—major violators, including violators from the ruling party. Second, after big fish are fried, anti-corruption efforts should focus on prevention. This includes selecting agents, changing incentives, enhancing accountability, enacting structural changes to mitigate monopoly and clarify discretion, and striving to increase the "moral costs" of corruption. Third, anti-corruption efforts should involve the people in many ways. They know where corruption resides. Give them a chance to tell. Under this rubric come such initiatives as hotlines for reporting corruption, citizen oversight boards, citizens' groups and NGOs to diagnose and monitor agency performance, village and barrio organizations to scrutinize public works, participation of accounting and lawyers groups, and so forth.

After finishing the second case, the participants turn to their own situation. The outside facilitator here asks them to go through the same headings as before: What kinds of corruption exist, which are more serious and which less, what are the alternatives and their pros and cons, and what tentative recommendations would they make. The subgroups go off and analyze, then present their results to the full group. A vivid discussion ensues, and the result is a tentative diagnostic of the types of corruption, their extent, their costs, and their possible remedies.

Before the workshop closes, the facilitator poses a final challenge. "This has been a fascinating exercise, but we don't want it to be just another workshop. What has to happen in the next six months, what concrete steps by this group, to move things forward?"

In our experience, the results have been remarkable. A fascinating and practical agenda usually emerges. What are sometimes lacking are the resources, the expertise, and the leverage to carry out that agenda. Here municipal leaders, perhaps with external assistance, may propose a special project to follow such an

Box 7: Participatory Diagnosis in La Paz, 1985

Result of Diagnostic Meetings in Late 1985 with Officials of the Municipal Government of La Paz, Bolivia

Type	Value	Who Is Helped	Who Is Hurt	Causes	Cures
Tax Evasion (all kinds)	US$20 million–US$30 million	Evaders	Recipients of city services; non-evaders; future Paceños	Hard to pay; taxes too high; low penalties; no reviews of cases	Make easier to pay; lower rates; raise penalties and enforce them; review cases
Tax "arrangements" (all kinds)	US$5 million–US$10 million	Corrupt taxpayers and officials	Recipients of city services; non-evaders; future Paceños	Lack of computerization; low effective penalties; no reviews; pay through municipality; low pay	Computerize; raise penalties; review cases; pay through banks; raise pay; raise incentives to collect
Extortion	US$0.5 million–US$1 million	Corrupt officials	Direct victims	Difficult rules, rates, and procedures; hard-to-report extortion; low penalties; no reviews; low pay	Simplify rules, rates, and procedures; hotline for public reports; raise penalties; review cases; pay through banks; raise pay
Speed money	US$0.5 million–US$1 million	Some taxpayers; corrupt city officials; substitutes for higher pay	Most taxpayers via slowdowns; reputation of city government	Difficult procedures; lack of computerization; pay through municipality; low penalties; no surveillance; low pay	Simplify procedures; computerize; pay through banks; raise penalties; surveillance and "whistle-blowing"; raise pay
Theft (city property, parts, cash)	US$0.5 million–US$1 million	Thieves	Recipients of city services	Lack of inventories; poor decentralization; low penalties; no reviews or surveillance	Computerize inventories; decentralize responsibility; spot checks and surveillance
Procurement	US$0.5 million–US$3 million	Corrupt officials and winning suppliers	Recipients of city services	Lack of information on prices; no reviews; low penalties; low pay	Verify prices; review cases; raise effective penalties; raise pay of decision-making officials
"*Fantasmas*," late reporting to work	US$0.1 million–US$0.2 million	Malingerers	Morale and reputation of city government	No surveillance; low penalties	Surveillance; raise penalties and enforce them

event—or several such events at different levels of the public and private sectors. The ensuing initiative should use some of the workshop's recommendations, co-opt key participants as activists and monitors, and via carrots and sticks improve the chances that the anti-corruption effort succeeds.

Box 7 summarizes what might be called a "first cut" analysis of various kinds of corruption in La Paz in 1985. It is the result of several workshops for officials and politicians. This process helped generate frank analyses of sensitive policy issues, and it led to a number of suggestions for remedial measures that no outsider could have concocted.

TECHNICAL STUDIES AND EXPERIMENTS

Participatory diagnoses should involve workshops at several levels of city government (and from several viewpoints, including clients and stakeholders). Research can also be useful in galvanizing and guiding reform. Of particular interest are studies of systems of information and evaluation (extent, quality, how used and misused), analyses of actual and experimental incentive systems, and studies of relatively uncorrupted institutions or departments within the city, or perhaps elsewhere in the country in question.

Consultants can be useful in several ways (see Box 8). Nonetheless, studies involving expensive experts are often overdone. Typically, studies of municipal administration seem to proceed with three assumptions that diminish their effectiveness. First, they often assume that any reform deserving the name should involve massive changes across the entire civil service. A second assumption is that such reforms require comprehensive studies and blueprints. Third, because such studies are technically

Box 8: Some Advantages of Outside Consultants

The benefits of using consultants include: signaling management's dissatisfaction with "business as usual"; freeing management to perform other tasks; infusing new ideas; serving as a "lightning rod"; and giving the manager an outside confidant.

Three other advantages of consultants are germane for the municipal leader interested in preventing corruption.

1. **Expertise.** The consultant can offer expertise that may not exist in the city government. Examples include computer systems to detect and prevent fraud, specialized investigatory techniques, management systems, and procurement processes.
2. **Facilitation.** Participatory diagnosis is crucial. Its sensitivity usually means that an inside facilitator is inappropriate. Apart from expertise in facilitation, the consultant is insulated from the appearance of empire building.
3. **Cooperation.** In fighting corruption, many branches of the municipality must collaborate. An outsider may be perceived to be neutral enough, and should be chosen to be expert enough, to facilitate such sharing and cooperation.

complicated, municipal officials assume they must be undertaken by expensive experts, including foreign technical assistants.

We believe that a more useful approach allows "studies" carried out by officials and clients, followed by experiments. In our experience officials and clients understand well how corrupt systems work. They can be encouraged to share their knowledge without fear of recriminations—for example, through anonymous surveys or group work involving anonymous written contributions that are then discussed. We recommend that employees be involved centrally in the design (and, eventually, the evaluation) of experiments with new systems of information, incentives, and accountability. This is in stark contrast to their usually peripheral involvement in grand studies by outside experts.

As an example, consider incentive reforms designed to deal with two key factors behind corruption, namely paltry wages and the failure to link rewards to performance. The municipality might select a few key functions, such as revenue raising, auditing, and procurement. In each area, officials would be asked to work through the schematic outline in Box 9.

The results would then be reviewed in workshops. Depending on the outcomes, the municipality might initiate experiments based on the proposition(s) listed in Box 9. The incentives could include pay, but might also mean training, travel, professional recognition, reassignment, promotion, better working conditions, more independence, and so forth. Some of the incentives could be for individuals, but many would probably be for teams (offices, bureaus, and departments). Such radical experiments would be facilitated by technical studies, as described in Box 10.

An example of a highly desirable study is what has become known as a "vulnerability assessment." Here employees themselves or outside experts, or both, take a systematic look through

Box 9: Model Memorandum for Employees, as the Basis for Incentive Experiments

1. **Quantitative summary of the current unsatisfactory situation.** Because of *X, Y, Z* shortcomings (resources, incentives, capabilities), we are currently able to process only *A*% of the cases we should; and of those, only *B*% are processed adequately. As a result the city's government and its citizens forgo ________ benefits and incur ___________ costs.
2. **Examples.** Here are three recent examples of what we were unable to do that clearly led to forgone benefits or additional social costs.
3. **Measures of success.** After considering our objectives and our organization's key tasks, here are the measures of performance by which we believe it is fair that we be assessed. For example:

    - quantitative measures of (a) activities undertaken and (b) results achieved;
    - estimates of the quality of a sample of activities by peer group, outsiders, or clients, on the proviso that ratings also include "grades on a curve" so that not every person and activity is deemed "excellent";
    - statistical controls that "adjust" measures of performance to take account of the relative difficulty of the target group one is working with (for example, for tax collectors, which suburb, type of economic activity, type of tax, and so on, all of which affect the amount earned);
    - performance-based contests among employees; and
    - measures of staff morale and turnover.

4. **Proposition.** If we had *x, y, z* (additional resources, incentives, capabilities), we will with *K* time period be able to achieve the following measurable (even if qualitatively) benefits and reductions in costs: *1, 2, 3, 4,* etc. We are willing to make such-and-such of the incentives conditional on the attainment of so-and-so performance targets, which will be monitored in the following transparent ways: *i, ii, iii, iv,* etc.

Box 10: Examples of Technical Studies to Help Prepare Incentive Reforms

1. Summarize information about current pay scales and work conditions, especially for key technical jobs and top managerial functions. Examples of data that would be relatively easy to collect: numbers of people leaving their jobs, of posts vacant, and of underqualified people employed in higher skilled jobs; compare pay and fringe benefits of recent hires in the private and public sector for people with roughly equal levels of qualifications. Look especially at key positions in revenue raising, auditing, accounting, management, procurement, and investigation. Compare with other public sector and private sector employment.
2. Analyze the distortions occasioned by current "tricks" to take advantage of per diems and other benefits accruing to travel, training, board membership, task forces, and so forth. Suggest remedies. Possible method: interviews with twenty-five top officials; review of detailed budgets to estimate amounts now spent by unit and level of employee on per diems, travel, training, allowances, and so forth.
3. Develop data about existing performance contracts in the city and in the country's public enterprises, including amounts expended, performance increments, how the moving goalposts were avoided, and political backlash (including resentment of their high pay). Derive lessons for experiments in the municipality.

Box II: Outline for a "Vulnerability Assessment"

A. Is the general control environment permissive of corruption?
   1. To what degree is management committed to a strong system of internal control?
   2. Are appropriate reporting relationships in place among the organizational units?
   3. To what degree is the organization staffed by people of competence and integrity?
   4. Is authority properly delegated—and limited?
   5. Are policies and procedures clear to employees?
   6. Are budgeting and reporting procedures well specified and effectively implemented?
   7. Are financial and management controls—including the use of computers—well established and safeguarded?

B. To what extent does the activity carry the inherent risk of corruption?
   1. To what extent is the program vague or complex in its aims; heavily involved with third-party beneficiaries; dealing in cash; or in the business of applications, licenses, permits, and certifications?
   2. What is the size of the budget? (The bigger the budget, the greater the possible loss.)
   3. How large is the financial impact outside the agency? (The greater the "rents," the greater the incentives for corruption.)
   4. Is the program new? Is it working under a tight time constraint or immediate expiration date? (If so, corruption is more likely.)
   5. Is the level of centralization appropriate for the activity?
   6. Has there been prior evidence of illicit activities here?

C. After preliminary evaluation, to what extent do existing safeguards and controls seem adequate to prevent corruption?

Source: Adapted from Office of Management and Budget (OMB), *Internal Control Guidelines* (Washington, D.C.: OMB, December 1982), Chap. 4.

an organization, a process such as procurement or hiring consultants, or an activity such as city works. Box 11 provides an outline for such a study.

INVOLVING THE PRIVATE SECTOR AND CITIZENS

The private sector has an important but often ignored role to play in fighting corruption. After all, it usually takes two to tango: For every government official receiving a bribe, someone in the private sector offers it. The private sector and citizens can help by supplying information about transgressions, by diagnosing inefficient and corrupt systems, and by helping police their own behavior.

Citizens' groups are becoming more active in the fight against corruption. An example is Transparency International, the non-government organization founded in Berlin in 1993 "to do for corruption what Amnesty International does for human rights." TI has designed a straightforward code of conduct (no bribery, honest bids, and so forth), which builds on previous work by the International Chamber of Commerce and the United Nations. In Ecuador, TI and the government have applied this code of conduct to both government officials and the private firms that compete for public contracts. The firms promise not to offer bribes, and government employees promise not to solicit or accept them. Notice that firms have an interest that others do not pay bribes. Thus, firms that sign this code of conduct might band together in their own interest to regulate themselves—if penalties and a mechanism for investigation can also be put in place.

This leads to an interesting idea for city governments. Suppose the city requires all firms doing business with the city to sign a code of conduct. Then, if one business believes that another has won a contract through bribery, the aggrieved business can call on

Box 12: Bangalore's Report Card on Municipal Services

A nongovernmental organization in Bangalore, India, recently completed an innovative "report card" on how well various municipal agencies were doing, in the eyes of citizens. A variety of information-gathering devices was used, ranging from surveys to key informant interviews to studies of objective measures of agency performance. Among the topics dealt with was corruption. For example, in what percentage of cases did a citizen have to pay a bribe to receive a municipal service? Widespread corruption was documented; and the annual costs of corruption, admittedly difficult to gauge, exceeded the entire municipal budget by a factor of seven.

The results were controversial but had a galvanizing effect on municipal leaders and the agencies involved. More important perhaps, the study serves as a baseline for further involvement of citizens in telling municipal agencies how well they are progressing.[a]

Note: a. Samuel Paul, "Evaluating Public Services: A Case Study on Bangalore, India," *New Directions for Evaluation*, American Evaluation Association, no. 67, Fall 1995.

the other signers of the code of conduct and the city government to investigate. At the same time that the alleged transgression is investigated, a broader study should be undertaken of the class of actions of which the transgression is an instance. For example, if the alleged bribery takes place in procurement, the study interviews an array of private firms on a confidential basis and develops a description of how the system of procurement currently works, and whether corruption exists. The study also makes recommendations for change. The results of both investigations would be published, although they would not have the force of law.

Adopting a simple code of conduct—one that is readily understandable by civil servants, the press, and the public—can be a valuable part of a campaign against corruption. It can be especially useful if there are mechanisms for the private sector to create and enforce binding norms.

Finally, the citizenry can help fight corruption in many ways. The greatest enemy of corruption is the people. Citizens are wonderful sources of information about where corruption occurs. The mechanisms include systematic client surveys, focus groups, hotlines, call-in shows, village and borough councils, citizen oversight bodies for public agencies, the involvement of professional organizations, educational programs, and so forth.

Box 12 provides an example from Bangalore, India. There, a nongovernment organization used a variety of mechanisms of citizen feedback, ranging from client surveys to focus groups, to create a "report card" on municipal services. The study and follow-ups to it helped galvanize greater municipal efficiency and locate particularly bad areas of corruption.

Ronald MacLean-Abaroa describes one example of how popular participation led to improved decisions and reduced corruption in La Paz:

Every year the mayor must present the city's operational budget to the city council. In the budget, priorities are set for the public works over the coming year. Of course, each urban improvement has an impact not only on the well-being of the citizens in the particular area where construction takes place, but also affects and improves the real estate value of the properties and land in that neighborhood.

I soon learned that the funds available to the city for infrastructure were woefully insufficient to meet the multiple needs of the neighborhoods. Therefore, I needed a strategy for setting priorities among the many competing demands. During the first years of my administration, my technical staff developed and presented to me a selection of public works and locations. That selection left the majority of the citizens unhappy, especially the poorer ones who lived far from the center of town and lacked almost everything. These people were not prepared to wait passively for promised improvements to materialize years later.

The first summer of my tenure, and every summer thereafter, I recruited a group of advanced graduate students, mostly from Harvard University and the Massachusetts Institute of Technology (MIT) in the United States, to come to La Paz to work with me. I posed the problem to them, and together we developed a decision model using several weighted variables to assign priorities to the set of public works that gave the city the greatest value added. For instance, the model assigned greater importance (weighted more heavily in analytic terms) to projects that benefited larger numbers of people, poor people, and children. To my surprise, projects which were comparatively low in the list of priorities presented to me by my technical department jumped ahead dramatically in priority under the model's multivariate evaluations. It seemed that, without increasing outlays, the city could reach many more people, extend them greater benefits, and increase their well-being.

Some months into my tenure as mayor, I had started to conduct citywide polls to determine our most urgent needs as perceived by the citizens themselves. Some general correlations were found with the Harvard-MIT model, but I still believed I needed additional information before establishing final priorities and releasing construction funds. So, we devised a questionnaire that listed the specific public works proposed by the municipality's technical office and distributed it to the "barrios," asking the neighbors to assign their own priorities to these public works and make any comments regarding these or other projects they find more important for their barrio.

To preserve anonymity, we distributed "suggestion boxes" around the city. Although we did not have what I regarded as a "satisfactory" number of responses, the many we did have did not necessarily resemble the order of priorities suggested by the technical staff or the cost-benefit choices of the model. Instead, many expensive works on the staff's list which had in turn been relegated to much lower priority by the model were not even mentioned or received few marks in the anonymous citizen responses to the questionnaire.

As a consequence, I decided to make a personal inspection of the sites of these suspicious works. To my surprise, they were for the most part located in sparsely populated areas, and seemed designed more to expand the city than provide services for existing neighborhoods. Moreover, during some of my surprise inspections, I found municipal machinery and employees constructing new streets and other works that were not included in the list of municipal building programs. Only then did it become clear to me that medium-level personnel of the municipality, usually with direct control over machinery and labor, had developed their own agenda and priorities to construct public works that were neither preferred by the citizens nor rated highly in the cost-benefit model.

These works were accomplished in exchange for "favors"—otherwise known as bribes—offered either by a group of neighbors or by individuals who were speculating on land and would collude with city employees and technicians whom they paid with land in the same area where they completed urban improvement projects. In some cases, the neighbors in poor areas had to pool their money to have urgently needed urban improvements made in their barrio, in direct disregard for the formally approved operating budget for public construction. In many cases, middle-level technical bureaucrats decided where and when to do what public works in exchange for favors, bribes, or in-kind transfers (usually land). In the eyes of the municipal engineers and technicians who engaged in these corrupt activities, this scheme compensated them (and then some!) for their barely subsistence wages (US$15–30 per month). In fact, it transformed some of them into prosperous land barons and real estate speculators.

This corrupt system was eliminated by contracting out public works under a step-by-step, incentive-based contracting process that links payments to satisfactory completion of project milestones. It was the participation of the people, through questionnaires and direct contact in their own neighborhoods, that made possible the detection of the corrupt exchange of public works for property or side payments.

Thus, introducing reliable information, analysis, and policy formulation on the supply side and encouraging and ensuring the participation of citizens from the demand side to help calibrate and correct the results of the supply-side work led to a much-improved system for delivering public goods and services.

Implementing Reform

ORGANIZE THE FIGHT AGAINST CORRUPTION

After using the various assessment techniques in Chapter 4, let us suppose we now have a good understanding of the types and levels of corruption we are confronting. We would then work through the framework of Chapter 3 (Boxes 4 and 5) with our staff to brainstorm the possible costs and benefits of different actions. We would begin to locate areas where the costs of corruption seem high and the costs of the remedial actions seem relatively low—and that is where we would be tempted to begin.

But before we do, we must analyze both the problems and the alternatives from the perspective of implementation. We need to work through the political, bureaucratic, and personal aspects of an anti-corruption effort. One of the political dimensions is how to use the battle against corruption as the lever for transforming city government, and not turn it into the generator of more red tape and delays.

For good and bad reasons, issues of who's in charge loom large in government. Preventing corruption and deterring it require the combined excellence of many government agencies. Of course every part of the city government has its own responsibilities of management, incentives, and control. But several functions have anti-corruption roles that cut across the others. Many of these are not inside the city government but outside (as in many countries is the case of the police) or, so to speak, above the city government at the prefectural, county, provincial, and national levels. Consider what functions would have to work well to prevent corruption. There would be accounting and auditing functions, some of which in most Latin American countries fall under the "Contraloría." To this, one would add police (often local, sometimes national under the Ministry of the Interior), prosecutors, courts at various levels, and the government ministry in charge of administration. One would also include the city council and perhaps the state or federal legislature. Revenue-raising functions are important, as are the bodies that carry out public works. Regulatory functions come in many varieties. The list could go on, and the lines are not clear across these areas. What is evident, however, is that investigating, prosecuting, and obtaining convictions will not succeed unless a number of government agencies work together. Neither will many preventive measures. Let us call this the problem of coordination.

Experience suggests that there is a second need in campaigns against corruption: a focal point. Someone, or some official body, has to be in charge of a campaign against corruption—has to have the political authority, be in the public eye, and possess the personal accountability. But at the same time, because no single agency can do everything in the fight against corruption and therefore a coordinated effort is required, the official body has to be above all a facilitator of joint action, a mobilizer of the resources of many agencies of government. It cannot be a boss, in other words.

A key political question concerning the implementation of an anti-corruption strategy is what sort of coordinating authority this should be. Several answers are possible, and there is no one right answer for all settings. Hong Kong's Independent Commission against Corruption, which we examined in Chapter 2, is one prototype. It is a kind of *super agency* against corruption. It combines investigation (like a police force), prevention (like a management consulting agency), and popular participation (like a community relations office). Its powers are huge. So is its budget and ability to hire excellent staff—not only investigators and enforcers, but also accountants, economists, management experts, systems analysts, lawyers, and others.

There are examples of municipal units with wide-ranging powers, although not as grand as the ICAC's. Box 13 outlines an interesting example from New York.

A second idea is an interagency *coordinating body*. Cities are not countries, of course, and municipal leaders will not be able to control many of the agencies that matter. Still, it may be possible to prompt the important agencies together to improve the coordination of their work.[1]

In 1992 Robert Klitgaard spent some time in Venezuela with the many agencies involved in the fight against corruption at the national level: the police, the Contraloría, the prosecutors, the Supreme Court (which administers all the courts), and finally the cabinet. The various agencies guarded their autonomy and did not want to meet in joint workshops—each wanted its own. Each agency's staff told in its workshop the most extraordinary stories about how its own good efforts had been thwarted by the incompetence and, yes, the corruption of the other agencies. They noted how cases would disappear in the cracks along their theoretical path from gathering information to investigation to prosecution to judicial decision. The blame was differently apportioned by these agencies, but two results were universally

Box 13: An Independent Office to Fight Corruption in New York City's School Construction

In 1989, New York City's newly created School Construction Authority was faced with rampant corruption in the multibillion-dollar school construction program (bid-rigging, price fixing, illegal cartels, racketeering, bribery, extortion, and fraud) in the city's construction industry. Its response was to form an Inspector-General Office (OIG). Through institutional reform of the business practices of the authority, the OIG has "fried some big fish," including employees of the Board of Education and the authority itself; banned over 180 firms from competing for school construction contracts; saved millions of dollars for the authority; and even prompted internal reforms in the supplier side of the industry.

Its key organizing principles include:

1. Responsibility for combating corruption does not lie with law enforcement authorities alone. Managers and procuring officials must become proactive and must integrate their work with law enforcement agencies. Nonjudicial administrative sanctions short of criminal charges are effective.
2. Many disciplines must collaborate if corruption is to be deterred in the first instance, detected and prosecuted when deterrence fails, and punished in a criminal trial to ensure credibility. These disciplines include lawyers, investigators, accountants, analysts, engineers, and experts in management theory and public administration.
3. The organization (in this case, the OIG) must be external to the School Construction Authority to preserve independence and autonomy. Communications with the authority would occur informally through day-to-day collaboration and formally through a senior position within the authority. Importantly, vesting one organization with the authority to combat corruption avoids the trap to which so many anti-corruption efforts fall prey: imposing additional rules and regulations as well as multiple layers of

oversight that in turn "contribute to organizational paralysis and dysfunctional conflict, thereby ironically increasing incentives [and opportunities] for corrupt payments. . . ."

Deterrence (including financial recoveries) and opportunity blocking were the primary methodological ideas underpinning the OIG's efforts.

1. **Deterrence**

   Criminal prosecutions, using undercover agents, search warrants, wiretaps, and covert surveillance, with severe fines and incarceration as predictable results.

   Civil prosecutions, with severe financial penalties (forfeiture, treble damages, injunctive relief).

   Administrative sanctions, primarily banning firms from competing for school construction contracts, hitting the firms that have a culture of corruption where it hurts the most—in the pocketbook. (Happily and predictably, other public agencies often follow these sanctions and debar the same companies.)

2. **Opportunity blocking**

   Debarments, advisories, and certifications. Debarments block a firm from bidding on construction contracts. Advisories warn project managers about improprieties suspected in a particular vendor. Certifications required of the principals of some firms set the stage for rescinding contracts and recovering full monetary restitution if subsequent events show contract award was based on fraudulent inducement.

   Independent auditing firm or private-sector Inspector-General. Funded by firms in cases in which adequate evidence exists for criminal prosecution but the public good mandates contracts not be suspended or the company banned, these independent bodies, selected by the OIG, monitor a vendor's performance.

   Other initiatives. These include: vulnerability assessments to identify weaknesses in the authority's business practices and contracting procedures; a Fair and Ethical Business Practice provision for contracts; and privatized labor law enforcement, paid for by offending vendors, to monitor violations of prevailing wage laws.

The primary tool that has led to the OIG's success is an elaborate bidder **prequalification process**. Each vendor that wants to bid on school construction contracts must complete a comprehensive (forty-page) questionnaire that looks at traditional measures such as financial assets and wherewithal and experience as well as at the key people associated with and running the company. Prequalification has given the OIG access to information not traditionally available except through difficult and time-consuming law enforcement procedures.

cited: widespread corruption, and terrific demoralization within each agency.

Before and after the workshops, Klitgaard met with the heads of these agencies—the ministers and chief justice and Contralor General—and he also met with the Venezuelan cabinet. They agreed with the diagnosis of their senior civil servants. They also agreed to set up two interagency coordinating bodies. One was at the ministerial level; another was at the director-general or top civil servant level. Among the missions of the second coordinating body was to track important cases through the system. Both committees also worked on systematic issues: preventive measures, for example, and the closer coordination of their anti-corruption efforts.[2]

Within a year, these coordinating bodies logged dramatic successes. Individual agencies learned through their cooperation how to improve not only coordination but their individual operations. Discussing their work together forced each agency to confront the others' perceptions of its work. Seeing ourselves through others' eyes can be a shock, but it can also be what finally motivates us to improve. Soon, many more anti-corruption cases were moving through the system. One of them was a very big fish indeed: President Carlos Andres Pérez, who was impeached.

In 1995 Colombia introduced a version of a coordination model, which had some interesting features in theory. There was one coordinating body in government and a second that involved something like the Hong Kong idea of a citizen oversight board. In the latter, seven citizens of distinction were to serve as a kind of interlocutor between the public and the governmental coordinating body. They were to relay complaints and diagnostic studies from the private sector and civil society to the governmental coordinating body, and they were then supposed to follow up to see what happened to those complaints. They also were supposed to oversee the government's anti-corruption activities, from the level of high strategy to that of particular actions. The hoped-for result would be much greater efficiency, transparency, and credibility in the fight against corruption.

As it happened, the coordinating body never lived up to expectations. President Ernesto Samper was himself subjected to charges of corruption, and in the turmoil the coordinating body proved virtually moribund. When President Andrés Pastrana took office in 1998, he promised to fight corruption. But the coordinating body still did almost nothing.

In the summer of 1999, the Colombian government announced a "presidential program of fighting against corruption."[3] Based in the office of the vice president, the program hopes to coordinate the activities of a number of Colombian government agencies and to obtain the cooperation of business groups and civic organizations. The program itself includes units for the formation of ethical values, for the strengthening of citizen participation in social control, for efficiency and transparency, and for investigation and sanction. No citizen oversight board is mentioned.

The first problem, then, is to organize a government's fight against corruption. The principles seemingly conflict: coordination and a focal point. Someone has to be in charge of the anti-corruption drive, but the drive will only succeed if the efforts of many agencies can be coordinated.

The next question is how to get started. Where should the effort begin?

PICK LOW-HANGING FRUIT

In addressing this question, let us suppose that municipal leaders have followed the steps of Chapters 3 and 4. They have applied the formula $C = M + D - A$ and used the framework for policy analysis (Box 4) to stimulate reflection on the kinds of anti-corruption measures that might be employed for various kinds of corruption. They have assessed their organizations and estimated the extent and impact of different sorts of corruption. They have recognized that not all kinds of corruption are equally harmful or equally easy to prevent. They have combined economic analysis with political assessment. They have asked, "What kinds of corruption hurt the most, and whom? What ways of fighting corruption are most effective, and what are the direct and indirect costs?"

Such analyses should focus on the externalities and incentives generated by corrupt activities of various kinds, not the amounts of money that change hands. As they used to say of government officials in Mexico, "They waste a million to steal a thousand." Of particular importance is corruption that undercuts financial and banking systems or systems of justice. The indirect negative effects of corruption can be huge here. The same is true for corrupt activities that lead to policy distortions. The importance of basic services makes them candidates for special examination, particularly as they are affected by systems of procurement, eligibility for benefits, and distribution.

After all the analysis, there is a simple rule for where to begin: "Pick low-hanging fruit." That is, select a type of corruption where visible progress might be made soon, without too great a cost. This advice runs counter to some reformers' instincts to do everything at once, or to tackle the kind of corruption with the most serious costs (which may also be the most difficult and protracted battle and therefore not the place to begin).

Sometimes the rule will be slightly different. For reasons of politics or simply to generate support, we may wish first to attack the kinds of corruption that are most obvious to citizens or most hated by them, or that seem to them the most urgent. For political reasons, it is good to begin an anti-corruption campaign where citizens perceive it to be most evident and most annoying, or where the political leadership has given a field particular salience, or where it is believed that corruption is undercutting economic reform.

Mayor MacLean-Abaroa describes an example of "low-hanging fruit" in La Paz in 1985.

Perhaps the most evident and generalized form of corruption occurred in the corridors and the main hall of the municipality. Hundreds of citizens wandered through, trying to complete some paperwork or make a tax payment. Because of the total disorganization and the lack of information for citizens, there emerged dozens of "tramitadores" who offered their services to "arrange" a citizen's paperwork or permit problems.

The first extortion of citizens occurred when they delivered their documents to these tramitadores. Then, when the paperwork was finished, very often illegally, the citizen was required to pay a "recognition," in addition to the official cost of the transaction. Receipts even for the official sums were infrequent, and it was clearly the case that much of the money was stolen by corrupt officials. What citizens did get was basically a kind of temporary "protection" from being molested by inspectors and the like.

The first step we adopted was to isolate those doing the paperwork from the public. We did not permit tramitadores or anyone else to wander freely from desk to desk "running signatures" and stamps. All transactions had to be deposited in a single place and be given a control number. They had to be picked up a few days later from another place. The functionaries who processed these transactions were kept practically secluded on the second floor of the municipality, where they had no way of "conversing" with the clients.

To complement this step, we opened accounts in the banking system so that tax payments could be made directly and municipal cashiers couldn't profit from a "float" to speculate in the black market with dollars, which was then common.

These simple measures didn't cut the grand corruption, but they did eliminate a major source of abuse and discretion that affected many citizens. Within a few weeks one could walk the corridors of city hall without colliding with hundreds of anxious and confused citizens, victims of extortion and veiled threats. Citizens found it easier to find out where their transaction was in the system, through a computer-based central registry of transactions. They could perceive that the situation had changed for the better.

ALIGN WITH FAVORABLE FORCES

It is important for city leaders to search for allies and for ways to align the anti-corruption efforts with broader forces in the society. Three examples illustrate the point.

First, suppose the national government is pushing market reforms and privatization. It will then be useful to emphasize these elements of one's anti-corruption strategy, in order to get national-level support and financing. Or if the federal government is currently stressing a battle against organized crime, the municipal government might give special attention to areas of municipal corruption where organized crime is suspected of playing a major role.

Second, the private sector and civil society may already have ready allies for an anti-corruption effort. Perhaps there is a chapter of Transparency International, whose support and expertise can be requested. Perhaps the local organization of accountants or lawyers or business executives has made corruption an issue. Perhaps civic leaders, nongovernment organizations, student groups, or labor unions have recently complained of fraud or extortion or kickbacks and can instantly be brought into the campaign. We may choose where to begin depending in part on what kinds of corruption these allies have placed high on their agendas and where they can be most helpful in reducing corruption.

Third, international organizations may play an important role in municipal works or in the move to decentralized government. Many of them have placed the fight against corruption high among their priorities, and it may be that special sources of support are available if municipal leaders seek them out. For example, a foreign aid agency may be interested in financial management. Our city may volunteer to be a test case of reform. Aid agencies also may have specific expertise that can be mobilized, such as procurement, taxation, or systematic client surveys.

RUPTURE THE CULTURE OF IMPUNITY

Another aspect of implementation involves breaking out of a culture of impunity, where citizens become jaded and defeatist. Here is an example from a newspaper column in Guatemala:

> *When in a society the shameless triumph; when the abuser is admired; when principles end and only opportunism prevails; when the insolent rule and the people*

tolerate it; when everything becomes corrupt but the majority is silent . . . [The laments go on for the entire piece, which then concludes:] When so many "whens" unite, perhaps it is time to hide oneself; time to suspend the battle; time to stop being a Quixote; it is time to review our activities, reevaluate those around us, and return to ourselves.[4]

When corruption has become systematic, we must attack the pernicious perception that *impunity* exists. Without doing so, our efforts to fight corruption and improve governance may not be taken seriously. The public has grown cynical about corruption. Citizens and bureaucrats have heard all the words before. They've even seen a few minor prosecutions. But a culture of corruption may remain, especially the feeling of high-level impunity.

Fry Big Fish

To break through this culture of corruption, experience indicates that *frying big fish* is essential. Big, corrupt actors must be named and punished so that a cynical citizenry believes that an anti-corruption drive is more than words. It is also important that a campaign against corruption is not confused with a political campaign, or a campaign against the opposition. Importantly, therefore, one of the first big fish should preferably come from the political party in power.

Here are some examples. In the case of Hong Kong, credibility for the new Independent Commission against Corruption came when the ex-police chief of Hong Kong was extradited from retirement in England and punished in Hong Kong. The ICAC also nailed the ex–number two and scores of other high-ranking police officials. To a skeptical public and a hardened civil service, frying these big fish sent a credible signal: "The rules of the game really have changed." As a former ICAC commissioner wrote:

> *An important point we had to bear in mind (and still have to) is the status of people we prosecute. The public tends to measure effectiveness by status! Will they all be small, unimportant people, or will there be amongst them a proportionate number of high-status people? Nothing will kill public confidence quicker than the belief that the anti-corruption effort is directed only at those below a certain level in society.*[5]

Italy's unprecedented success in attacking corruption has attracted worldwide attention. A crucial step was frying a top Mafia official, many top business executives, and several major politicians from the ruling party. This told citizens that if they came forward and denounced crime and corruption, they could make a difference.

In the case of La Paz, Mayor MacLean-Abaroa quickly moved against the corrupt cashier.

> *In city hall in 1985, the cashier was a mixture of Robin Hood and the godfather. He would loan money to employees and perhaps help them with illicit supplements to their meager pay. I was told that he even "advanced" funds to the mayor, when for example an urgent trip came up and the usual processes for obtaining money were thought too slow. As I mentioned earlier, the cashier himself lived like a king. He was thought to be an untouchable because of his services in the municipality and his excellent connections in the treasury of the nation.*

I realized that it was necessary to give a very visible signal that the old order was over and that the new democratically elected authority was not willing to go along with corruption. The most conspicuous representative of the old order of corruption was the infamous cashier, whom we summarily dismissed to the astonishment and the not-very-timid opposition of many functionaries who assured me that the city couldn't work without the almost "magical" powers of this cashier.

The cashier's dismissal was the first of many other measures that followed, aimed at combating corruption.

Even though "frying big fish" is an indispensable step in breaking the culture of impunity, the emphasis on past offenders can be overdone. An analogy with health policy is germane. Individual cases of grave illness must be treated. But in the long run, prevention deserves priority. Therefore, after frying a few big fish, city officials must turn to prevention and the reform of institutions.

Make a Splash

An anti-corruption effort can garner credibility and publicity in many other ways. The mayor may call a "summit meeting" on preventing corruption. With careful advanced preparation, he may then announce a systematic program including revenue collection, public works, benefits, licenses and permits, and the police. He may invite the public to denounce corrupt acts and offer a variety of ways to do so. Then in the weeks and months to follow, again with careful prior preparation, he may announce the arrest of "big fish."

Here are other examples to illustrate making a splash to garner credibility. Each is based on a real, national-level example, here extrapolated to the municipal level:

1. The mayor organizes a high-level workshop for top municipal officials and leaders of the private sector and civil society to address corruption and what to do about it. From this event ideas will emerge, including a six-month action plan. This workshop might be followed by other seminars in various key departments, public works, and the police.
2. The mayor announces that all public officials will sign a standard of conduct that precludes the acceptance of bribes. At the same time, he says that no one will be allowed to bid on a public contract who has not signed a similar standard of conduct concerning the offering of bribes. The private sector will be enlisted to form an independent monitoring capability to investigate complaints. Organizations such as Transparency International should be approached for their support.
3. The mayor announces an experimental program within the city's revenue bureaus, whereby officials will be paid a proportion of additional tax revenues generated within the next two years. The bonus will amount to about 25–50 percent of existing pay and will only kick into play if revenues exceed a certain target increase (perhaps 25 percent). At the same time, officials will develop a performance evaluation system, where revenue targets are conditioned by region and activity and where non-revenue indicators of excellence and lack of abuse are included.
4. The mayor announces the creation of a Corruption Prevention Unit. With the help of international consultants, this office will review all bureaucratic procedures with an eye to reducing opportunities for

Box 14: Some New Laws That Would Help Reduce Corruption

Better laws can make a difference. Here are four examples, which go beyond the purview of a municipality's authority but would abet local campaigns to reduce corruption.

1. Financing political parties and campaigns

In many countries campaign financing involves coerced payments, and sometimes straight graft. When such behavior becomes systematic, even an "honest" political party may feel compelled by the corruption of its competitors to shake down businesses with implicit promises or threats. Parties may use their members in municipalities to siphon off public funds for their political war chests. In some countries, parties and local politicians set up local "foundations" and nongovernment organizations into which public funds for "local development" can be channeled, without the usual government auditing procedures.

Pressures for these sorts of corruption can be reduced through strict limits on campaign activities and party finances, both externally audited, coupled with public funding for campaigns and mandatory balanced-time allocations on television and radio. All foundations receiving public funds should be subject to audit.

2. Illicit enrichment

In some countries government officials can be prosecuted not only for direct evidence of having received a bribe—evidence which is always difficult to obtain—but also for possessing wealth beyond what can be explained as the result of lawful activities. Some countries have even reversed the burden of proof: A government official may be required to demonstrate that his wealth, and perhaps that of his immediate family, was acquired legally. In some countries there is no need to prove the individual is guilty of a crime.[a]

Note: a. A useful precedent internationally is the *United Nations Convention against Illicit Traffic in Narcotic Drugs and Psychotropic Substances* (The United Nations, E/CONF.82/15 and Corr. 1 and 2. See especially Article 5, Section 7.) The principle of forfeiture of assets applies, with the onus of proof on the accused. Because of possible abuses with regard to accusations of corruption, this reversal of the onus of proof probably should be restricted to the evidence and be made rebuttable.

Illicit enrichment laws carry risks. The power to demand proof can be misused. Excellent potential candidates for public office may be deterred by the possibility of having to open up their finances and the finances of their families to public scrutiny. In very corrupt situations such a law may simply drive corrupt officials to hide their wealth in secure places beyond the country's borders. Nonetheless, in Hong Kong the leverage obtained by a change in the law concerning illicit enrichment helped turn around the battle against corruption, as part of a wider-ranging package that included prevention and public participation.

3. Disclosure

Sanctions by administrative authorities may not merely reinforce the threat of criminal prosecution but may constitute an even more credible threat. For example, if bribery reporting is made mandatory to regulatory and tax authorities, the prospects change. Compared with police, these agencies usually have access to better information and have more expertise. It is relatively easier for them to impose sanctions. Such agencies may also play on a divergence of interests within corporate structures (for example, auditors and board members who may be reform-minded or merely self-protective).

4. Structuring anti-corruption efforts

Some municipalities and departments have set up anti-corruption units; such units at the national level can abet a city's own efforts. On a less grand (and less expensive) scale, anti-corruption statutes may simultaneously (1) create an anti-corruption coordinator from among existing units, and (2) enable and require various kinds of coordinating mechanisms and oversight functions, to ensure that the different aspects of the effort are articulated and that the public has the ability to monitor what the anti-corruption effort entails.

There are many other examples of better laws that can help control corruption, such as when a flat tax or a simplified licensing law reduces the scope for illicit activities.

corruption and abuse: what the Hong Kong Independent Commission against Corruption calls "vulnerability assessment." The first agencies to be reviewed will be ones where the public perceives that corruption is systematic—for example, permit and licensing agencies, tax bureaus, procurement units, and so forth.

5. The mayor seeks ways to involve the public in the fight for good government, in the ways mentioned above.
6. The mayor designates teams of honest, senior civil servants and young, excellent university graduates to investigate reported instances of corruption and also to evaluate random samples of important cases of tax payments and exceptions, public procurement, and so forth.
7. The providers of city services are challenged to develop measures of success against which performance may be pegged and then to design an experiment linking increased compensation to such performance. The incentives would be paid on a group basis and again would be in the area of 25–50 percent of salaries for excellent performance. The sustainability of the experiment would depend on the prospect of user charges.
8. The mayor announces publicly that the city will conduct some number of procurement "sting" operations during the next year. Even if only a few such operations are carried out, as part of a package of initiatives this step could deter potential bribe-takers.

CHANGE SYSTEMS

Corruption is inherently precarious. "To engage in corruption," Philip Heymann notes, "a government official and a private party have to identify each other as potential corrupt partners, and find a way to reach an agreement, and then deliver what each has promised without being detected. Each of these steps can be extremely difficult, for in each there are vulnerabilities to detection."[6]

Corruption requires
1. finding corrupt partners
2. making payments
3. delivering what is corruptly purchased
all done inconspicuously

When corruption has become systematic, it means that opportunities have been identified and relationships established, that mechanisms for payment exist, and that deliveries are routinely made. These routines are difficult to establish. Collusion also requires formidable preconditions, as an analysis of auctions notes:

> *How do members know what objects to bid on at the main auction? How high should they bid? If an item is won by a member of the coalition, do they own it? Do they need to transfer moneys to members of the coalition? If an item won by a member belongs to the coalition, how is ultimate ownership determined? How is the realized collusive gain shared among ring members? What incentives are there for cheating on the collusive agreement? How can the coalition dissuade and/or monitor members to deter cheating?*[7]

One anti-corruption tactic is to analyze these corrupt routines and disrupt them. Corruption prefers a stable, secretive environment. By creating enough discontinuity, uncertainty, and distrust, we hope to reduce corruption.

What does such disruption require? To some the automatic answer is "new laws." In fact, systematic corruption often coexists with highly developed legal codes. Sometimes more rules and regulations not only strangle efficiency but actually create opportunities for corruption. New laws and rules are most welcome when they change incentives, reduce monopoly power, clarify or reduce discretion, and enhance information and accountability. Some examples of welcome new laws appear in Box 14, but in general we believe that new laws are not the automatic answer.

A more promising approach is to prevent corruption by changing the underlying conditions of competition, discretion, accountability, and incentives. This means the careful consideration of, for example:

1. Privatizing works or contracting them out, and focusing scarce municipal resources on inspection and monitoring of agreed-upon, measurable results.
2 Adopting "second-best" rules and regulations which, though not optimal in some theoretical world, serve to delineate discretion and make the rules of the game easy to understand. Disseminating the rules of the game to citizens can be a key step (see Box 15).
3. New sources of information about results, including peer reviews, citizens' evaluations, objective indicators, and the careful evaluation of samples of performance. The culture of nonperformance leads to low, unvarying wages, which breed corruption and inefficiency.
4. Innovative uses of computers to track possible beneficiary fraud, bid-rigging, underpayment of property taxes, and suspicious cost overruns or delays in public works.
5. Use of self-policing mechanisms by the private sector, as described earlier.
6. Radical experiments with incentives, also described earlier.

Box 15: A Citizens' Manual Helps Prevent Corruption

La Paz's municipal government was riddled with routine corruption in part because municipal rules and regulations were both extremely complex and not transparent to the public. Trying to figure out how to get a certain permit, for example, was virtually impossible. Routine purchases under $2,000 required twenty-six steps within the municipality. Municipal employees could use both the delays and the obscurity to request speed money or in some cases to extort citizens by pretending that the regulations were something they were not.

Municipal employees were asked to describe exactly what every procedure entailed. They resisted mightily, and the effort to document all the municipality's methods took over a year. Then two responses made a dramatic difference. First, the procedures were simplified. The twenty-six steps were cut to six. What had been supposed oversight and review of each and every case (necessarily cursory or nonexistent) became the careful review of a random sample of cases.

Second, the city published a citizens' manual describing all the procedures. For many citizens it was their first chance to get straightforward, objective information on municipal procedures and regulations.

La Paz used private banks instead of city cashiers for the payment of taxes and fees. It made radical cuts in the numbers of public employees in exchange for huge salary increases for those who remained. In a radical effort to cut collusion in the estimates of property taxes, a simple model was developed based on real estate market prices. Citizens were then asked to "auto-evaluate" their own property's value, with the veiled threat that houses might be purchased by the state if the value declared was too low. Citizens were provided with guidelines depending on the characteristics of their house and its location. Citizens cooperated: La Paz's property tax revenues soared even as corrupt arrangements were virtually eliminated.

Another example is the Bolivian national government's use of private agencies to evaluate bidders for public contracts. In fact, this process also fell afoul of charges of corruption. But the argument is that international firms with a reputation to uphold probably have a greater incentive to police potentially corrupt principal-agent relationships than do underdeveloped government agencies.

WORK WITH BUREAUCRACY NOT AGAINST IT

For systematic change to occur, municipal bureaucracies must be enlisted, mobilized, and monitored.

Begin with Something Positive

Experience teaches that it is unwise for municipal leaders to begin by seeming to attack their own officials and agencies, even if these are known to be vitiated. In the words of Justice Efren Plana, who successfully overcame systematic corruption in his wide-ranging reforms of the Philippines' Bureau of Internal Revenue: "You cannot go into an organization like the white knight, saying that everyone is evil and I'm going to wring their necks." He took positive steps to help his employees first—not incidentally developing new measures of performance.

To the extent they wouldn't put their heart into their work, or would pocket some of the money that should go to the government, then you don't get efficiency. So, we needed a system to reward efficiency. . . . So, I installed a new system for evaluating performance. I got the people involved in designing the system, those who did the actual tax assessment and collection and some supervising examiners.

Before, there was a personal evaluation by the supervisor, especially by the person who actually decided on the promotion. Now, instead of this, I introduced a system based on the amount of assessments an examiner had made, how many of his assessments were upheld, the amounts actually collected—all depending on the extent and type of the examiner's jurisdiction.[8]

Emphasize Information and Incentives

Crucial ingredients for galvanizing bureaucracies are new infusions of information about performance and new incentives linked to that information. Too many managers focus on administrative reform in terms of (a) reorganization or (b) adding competencies. Our contention is that when systematic corruption exists, neither step is likely to make much difference—unless what might be called the informational environment is radically altered and incentives (positive and negative) are transformed. In our judgment, as mentioned earlier, the best way to achieve these ends is with an experimental approach, one that involves the employees affected and that uses feedback from the city's clients and citizens.

Building better governments simply by trying to strengthen Western-style bureaucracies has failed in many developing countries. The *context* in many developing countries is not conducive to successful government institutions. For example:

1. Information and evaluation are scarce and expensive, which inhibits internal and external controls.
2. Information-processing skills are weak at both the individual and institutional levels, due for example to low levels of education and few computers, as well as to relatively few specialists such as accountants, auditors, statisticians, and so forth.
3. Incentives are weak, in the sense that good performance goes relatively unrewarded and bad performance relatively unpunished. Box 16 provides some practical advice for reforming incentive systems.
4. Political monopolies dominate, sometimes coupled with violence and intimidation.
5. Countervailing institutions are weak, in part because of information and incentives problems but also because of hostile actions by the state.
6. Consequently, good economic reasons explain the failure of government institutions to perform. One need not cite cultural or political factors, and one need not immediately turn there for solutions.

Correspondingly, the principles of reforming corrupt bureaucracies will include:

1. Enhance information and evaluation. Put it in the hands of clients, legislators, and those with official oversight (regulators, auditors, judges, and so on).

2. Improve incentives. Link incentives to information about the attainment of agreed-upon objectives.
3. Promote competition and countervailing forces—including civil society, the media, the legislature and the courts, and political parties—and procedures that allow these different interests and voices to make a difference in policy and management.

This approach contrasts with approaches based on *more:* more training, more resources, more buildings, more coordination, more central planning, and more technical assistance. The argument is that without systematic reforms, *more* won't solve the problem of inefficient, corrupt public administration in contexts like those found in many developing countries. In these senses, the fight against corruption can become the vanguard of a revolution in city governance.

Box 16: Some Practical Advice for Incentive Reforms

The first question is: Where do we get the money to increase pay? Mayor MacLean-Abaroa undertook radical cuts in personnel; many mayors will not have a crisis to defend such a step. Experiments that begin with the revenue-raising and cost-saving parts of the municipality can pay for themselves, and even generate revenues that can be used to fund a second round of incentive experiments elsewhere in city government. User charges can be shared with employees. Foreign aid money can sometimes be used for "topping up" the salaries of key personnel.

Incentive reforms require the participation of employees themselves in the specification of each agency's objectives, the definition of performance measures, and the structure of incentives.

Quantitative and qualitative outcome measures can be used. So can peer ratings, as long as ratings are forced to be "on a curve" (that is, not everyone can be rated "excellent").

Team incentives are often more feasible and desirable than individual incentives.

In designing performance measures, it is helpful to define "key tasks"—in other words, to analyze the organization's "production function" better.

Include information from clients.

Empower clients. Seek analogies to market power or joint management. In pursuing such reforms, continually think "information and incentives."

Experiment with user charges and analogies to them such as in-kind contributions, part of the revenues from which can be used to augment employees' salaries and benefits.

Remember the principle of the sample: Incentives can be based on samples of performance. Especially in an experiment, there is no need for the comprehensive measurement of each and every outcome of each and every action.

Avoid incentive master plans for all agencies and all time. Learn by doing. Make sure affected parties take part in the evaluation of the incentive experiments.

Begin with the easiest cases. In particular, try reforms in areas where performance is relatively easy to measure objectively and where the revenues raised or costs saved can make the experiment self-financing.

Incentives include money but also other rewards: promotions, training, travel, special assignments, transfers, awards, favorable recognition, and simple praise. Even information about how well one is doing turns out to function as an incentive.

Cultivate political support, particularly from unions and foreign donors. The idea of an experiment reduces their worries and involves them in design and evaluation.

Challenge technical assistance (TA) by foreigners. For example, use TA funds to finance experiments where local experts and even government officials carry out the required "studies" based on the participatory diagnosis of what is already known about problems and possible solutions.

Privatize creatively. This can mean experimenting with hybrids of public and private sectors working together to provide services.

CHAPTER 6

Conclusions and Extended Remarks

In this final chapter we review the main themes of the book and provide an overview of the steps municipal leaders might consider to reduce corruption. We then return to the case of La Paz, updating it to 1996. Corruption, severely pruned in the mid-1980s, has grown back. What does this suggest about the sustainability of anti-corruption initiatives?

AN EXAMINATION OF CORRUPTION

Corruption is the misuse of office for unofficial ends. The catalog of corrupt acts includes bribery, extortion, influence peddling, nepotism, fraud, speed money, embezzlement, and more. Although we tend to think of corruption as a sin of government, of course it also exists in the private sector. Indeed, the private sector is involved in most government corruption. We are all in this together, and together we must find a way out.

Different varieties of corruption are not equally harmful. Corruption that undercuts the rules of the game—for example, the justice system or property rights or banking and credit—devastates economic and political development. Corruption that lets polluters foul rivers or hospitals extort patients can be environmentally and socially corrosive. In comparison, some speed money for public services and mild corruption in campaign financing are less damaging.

Of course, the extent of corruption matters too. Most systems can withstand some corruption, and it is possible that some truly awful systems can be improved by it. But when corruption becomes the norm, its effects are crippling.

So, although every municipality and every country experience corruption, the varieties and extent differ. The killer is systematic corruption that afflicts the rules of the game. It is one of the reasons why the most underdeveloped parts of our planet stay that way.

What to do about systematic corruption? Both multiparty democracy and free-market reforms will help. Both enhance competition and accountability, and these in turn tend to reduce corruption. But democracy and freer markets are certainly not sufficient. Corruption tends to follow a formula: $C = M + D - A$ or corruption equals monopoly plus discretion minus accountability. Whether the activity is public, private, or nonprofit, whether we are in La Paz, Lilongwe, or Los Angeles, we will tend to find corruption when someone has monopoly power over a good or service, has the discretion to decide whether or not someone receives it and how much the person will get, and lacks accountability.

Corruption is a crime of calculation, not passion. True, there are saints who resist all temptation, and honest officials who resist most. But when the size of the bribe is large, the chance of being caught small, and the penalty if caught meager, many officials will succumb.

Solutions, therefore, begin with systems. Monopolies must be weakened or removed. Discretion must be clarified. Accountability must be strengthened. The probability of being caught must increase, and the penalties for corruption (both givers and takers) must rise. Incentives must be linked to performance.

Each of these headings introduces a vast topic, of course, but notice that none immediately refers to what most of us think of first when corruption is mentioned—new laws, more controls, a change in mentality, or an ethical revolution. Laws and controls prove insufficient when systems are not there to implement them. Moral awakenings do occur, but seldom by the design of our public leaders.

If we cannot engineer incorruptible officials and citizens, we can nonetheless foster competition, change incentives, and enhance accountability: In short, we can fix the systems that breed corruption.

We are not saying this is easy. But three points deserve emphasis. First, successful examples do exist of reducing corruption, at the level of firms, cities, projects, ministries, and entire countries. Second, many of these success stories contain common themes, which we shall review shortly. Third, the fight against corruption can be the leading edge of much broader and deeper reforms of municipal government. In addition, we suggest at the end of this chapter, if the fight against corruption does not lead to those broader and deeper reforms, corruption will tend to reemerge.

One successful example occurred in La Paz, Bolivia, beginning in 1985.

THE FIRST BATTLE OF LA PAZ

Most observers will agree that the situation in La Paz in 1985 was grave. The city had just experienced the first democratic election in forty years, with Ronald MacLean-Abaroa as the new mayor. Bolivia's hyperinflation had been stanched by a remarkable austerity program, but these welcome changes coincided with a city in crisis. As Mayor MacLean-Abaroa took office, the city's payroll was 120 percent of its revenues despite miserable wages eroded by the inflation: A city engineer might earn only US$30 per month, and the mayor's salary was a meager US$45 per month. Previous mayors had added more and more employees for political reasons. In 1985 the city employed about 5,700 people, 4,000 of whom were workers.

The municipal government was a cornucopia of corruption. Public works, carried out for the most part by the city, featured everything from theft of parts and fuel to fraudulent fulfillment of quality standards, in addition to great inefficiency. Tax collection was rife with "fixes" (a lower assessment on your house in exchange for a bribe) to speed money (the city collected taxes itself, and paying sometimes involved standing in long lines). Applications for permits and licenses were often delayed unless speed money was paid, and finally obtaining the permit or license often entailed another bribe. Procurement involved many arcane steps and little transparency, resulting in bribes and extortion to obtain a contract and then, after one performed the work, bribes in order to be paid. Personnel systems often worked on the basis of friendship or political influence; there was little tradition of professionalism. Auditing and investigations were lax and themselves subject to corruption. Finally, some senior executives and some city council members used their positions to move favored applications and vendors through the system, in exchange for monetary and other illicit considerations.

Needless to say, under these circumstances the city was failing in all its missions. Faced with such systematic corruption, many people would simply give up. Or they would call for institutional strengthening of what we call a "supply-side strategy"—in other words, for *more*: more training, more foreign experts, more computers, more regulations—and of course for a code of ethics and a recasting of attitudes.

Ronald MacLean-Abaroa's strategy was different, even though it also included supply-side elements. He understood that at the heart of institutional rot are broken-down systems of information and incentives. He took to heart the formula $C = M + D - A$.

Diagnosis

His first step was to undertake a number of diagnostic activities. Where was the corruption, how bad was it, what were its causes and possible cures? Workshops with senior officials, which we earlier called "participatory diagnosis," not only gathered useful information (Box 12) but also motivated these officials to devise their own strategies for reform. Special studies also helped, ranging from the highly informal (interviews with secretaries—a repository of institutional knowledge about transgressions) to systems analyses of procurement.

Strategy

After sizing up his daunting problems, Mayor MacLean-Abaroa applied an early version of the framework for policy analysis (Box 4) to each of the city's major activities (for example, works, revenue collection, permits and licenses, procurement, auditing, and evaluation). The city government undertook a number of impressive steps toward improvement.

Public works. The mayor used the city's financial crisis to defend the firing of large numbers of employees, particularly laborers in the public works area. He took this opportunity to redefine the city's mission as carrying out emergency repairs but not major projects. In the latter case, it would supervise but not undertake the works. Mayor MacLean-Abaroa obtained foreign aid for municipal works, most of which he applied directly to public works projects. (He used the remainder to help reform city administration, as the subsequent section on personnel discusses.)

Which city works projects should be built? Mayor MacLean-Abaroa used a variety of techniques to estimate the value of various kinds of public works projects to neighborhoods and to the city more generally. These techniques ranged from surveys of local groups to benefit-cost studies using high-powered outside advisers.

Revenue collection. Revenue collection was assigned to banks rather than city employees, reducing the scope for bribery and extortion by city officials. The complicated system for evaluating the value of property was replaced with an "auto-evaluation," wherein citizens would declare the value of their properties under the veiled threat that the city might purchase their properties at the value the citizens declared. The result was a remarkable increase in city revenues.

Permits and licenses. The mayor deregulated some activities, so that no permits were required and no bribes could be extorted. He abolished the office of price control.

He developed a single register of all applications for permits and licenses. Applicants would come to a desk staffed by registry employees, not by those actually evaluating and granting permits and licenses. Each application was entered into a system that enabled its progress to be monitored. The scope for bribe-taking was reduced, and the information gathered through the system could be used to help evaluate the performance of offices and individual employees. The system was never fully implemented, but it did make a difference.

He undertook a great effort to simplify and streamline the granting of permits and licenses. Then he published a "Manual for Paceños," which described each process in detail so citizens knew what to expect and were less easily extorted based on their ignorance.

For building permits, he created a plan to involve private sector architects under the aegis of the College of Architects. They would take some responsibility for reviewing and warranting the quality and legality of the construction plans. Adding more than 100 private sector architects would speed up approvals and improve the quality of the reviews.

Procurement. Systems that formerly took many steps, very difficult to monitor, were simplified to fewer steps, with more effort at monitoring carefully each step.

Personnel. Efforts were made to increase the professionalism of the city's staff through meritocratic recruiting and promotion. Young people were brought in under a plan called "Bolivia Jóven." Thanks to personnel cuts, enhanced revenues, and foreign aid, salaries were raised, to the point that within two years they were competitive with the private sector. By "topping up" the salaries of key officials, the city was able to attract real talent to the important jobs of planning and supervising municipal projects, especially in the area of public works. Training was radically increased, and a special program funded by the World Bank had as a central objective the upgrading of city personnel. A new Institute for Municipal Training was set up.

Auditing. A project was undertaken with a major consulting firm to design and implement an integrated financial management system, running from requests for materials and public works through their procurement, warehousing, and supervision. Unfortunately, this system was not completed before MacLean-Abaroa left office.

Implementation

Mayor MacLean-Abaroa followed a sensible implementation strategy as well. He aligned with favorable national and international forces. He "fried some big fish" early on, and used their example to send a message that the old corrupt systems had changed. He did not attack his bureaucracy but helped it first, then went after corruption through a preventive strategy involving the reform of systems of information, incentives, and competition. He recovered the city's memory. For example, he resuscitated a major study of the city's long-term needs for infrastructure. This plan, massively funded by the French government, had languished for eight years. It included large-scale studies that helped organize thinking about needed public works and services.

The results were remarkable. Within three years, investment in the city's infrastructure rose by a factor of ten. Revenues soared. Within two years, salaries in the city government were competitive with the private sector. By all reports, corruption was reduced. Subsequently, Mayor MacLean-Abaroa was reelected twice.

SUMMARY OF STEPS FOR FIGHTING CORRUPTION

Box 17 summarizes the steps to follow in an effort to prevent corruption. There is no rigid recipe here, rather a set of suggestions designed to stimulate new thinking by municipal leaders.

SUSTAINING REFORMS

After finishing the first draft of this book in August 1995, Ronald MacLean-Abaroa decided to run again for mayor of La Paz—in

Box 17: Recommended Steps in Preventing Corruption

1. Diagnose the types of corruption and their extent.
   a. Participatory diagnosis: workshops for those involved in corrupt systems.
   b. Systematic anonymous surveys of employees and clients.
   c. Special studies, including "vulnerability assessments."
2. Design a strategy focusing on systems. Use the framework for policy analysis (Box 4) to brainstorm possible options, their impact, and their direct and indirect costs. The broad headings are:
   a. Selecting agents.
   b. Setting rewards and penalties.
   c. Obtaining information about results.
   d. Restructuring the principal-agent-client relationship: Reduce monopoly, clarify and limit discretion, and enhance accountability.
   e. Raise the "moral costs" of corruption.
3. Develop an implementation strategy.
   a. Organize the government's efforts: coordination and a focal point.
   b. "Pick low-hanging fruit": Choose a relatively easy-to-fix problem first.
   c. Align with favorable forces (national, international, private sector, NGO).
   d. Break the culture of impunity by "frying big fish."
   e. Raise the profile of the anti-corruption effort through publicity.
   f. Do something good for government officials before seeming to attack them.
   g. Strengthen institutional capacity not only through "supply-side measures" (more training, more experts, or more computers) but especially through changing systems of information and incentives.

h. Consider how an anti-corruption campaign can galvanize broader and deeper changes in municipal government (such as client consultation, pay-for-performance, or privatization with high quality regulation).

this case as so often, however, chronology does not imply causality. In the November election, no candidate won a majority vote. MacLean-Abaroa defeated the incumbent mayor in a subsequent vote among the eleven elected city councilors. Upon assuming office in 1996, he invited Robert Klitgaard to La Paz for an assessment of the city's financial situation and a look at the overall municipal strategy. (Lindsey Parris was unable to come.) It had been four-and-one-half years since MacLean-Abaroa left the mayor's office, and two mayors had served in the interim. It was amazing how corruption had once again emerged.

A senior member of the mayor's staff said: "I know you all faced tremendous problems back in 1985 and things were quite bad then, but I think we have to begin from zero all over again. The situation is that bad.

"Just to give you an example, I would guess that 95 percent of the vehicles of the Alcaldía have the odometers and the speedometers and the starters broken. Why? So they can claim for gasoline. We spend a fortune on gasoline. Some of it is in ridiculously large allowances. My job, for instance, used to grant 600 liters of fuel per month. We've cut that down to 200 liters, and that's plenty. The city vehicles all want to look as though they've been running all the time. And everyone is claiming for overtime, and breakfasts and lunches because they're working."

There were worse examples of institutional decay.

Works. The Chamber of Construction, a group of private firms, had made public complaints in the previous administration concerning extortion. None had been heeded. According to some people inside the municipality, winning contracts requires a bribe of 10–15 percent. When public works are completed and payment is to be made, a bribe of 10 percent is often sought "for the [political] party." The threat of nonpayment is real, as the city's short-term debt including nonpayment had risen sharply in the previous two years. By 1996 the city was $20 million in arrears.

Tax collection. The "auto-evaluation" system eroded when it became clear that the city had no effective penalty for understating the value of one's property. (The threat to buy the property for a multiple of its declared value turned out to be illegal, and after a few years its credibility waned.) In 1995 a new system was installed that provided "automatic" valuations depending on self-declared housing characteristics. The result was a large number of much higher tax assessments for the poor and lower-middle class. Large protests followed, and thousands of individual complaints had to be addressed, usually by simply adjusting the assessment downward. Public anger continued, and one member of the previous administration believes that the bad taste of this episode led to the incumbent mayor's defeat. In any case, a form of tax evasion through under-declaration led to an estimated shortfall of at least 100 percent in property tax revenues.

Permits and licenses. The single registry for applications for permits and licenses and other transactions had broken down completely. The official in charge described, in a memorandum in February 1996, an "almost infinite" list of reasons, which revolved around the rapid rotation of officials seeking their own and their party's interest in obtaining bribes. It is now routine—"all the time, every day"—to pay speed money of B.200 (about US$40) for the "revision of paperwork."

The system of the architects' evaluating building plans was finally implemented, after being ready for four years. The architects still took a slice of the fee paid by all those seeking building permits, but apparently they simply checked that the square meters declared were correct (and that the correct fee was paid).

When asked to live up to the original agreement to confirm the quality and legality of the plans, the College of Architects now complained that it did not want corruption moved from the city government to the college. (However, the college did wish to continue receiving its allotment of funds.)

Procurement. Collusion had become common. Outsiders who submitted lower bids were rejected by corrupt municipal personnel according to vague standards of quality. As mentioned above, bid-padding coexisted with bribes at both the award and payment stages.

Personnel. Salaries remained relatively high, but pay and promotion were not linked with performance. Instead, political appointments were so common that an estimated 40 percent of managerial and technical employees had been replaced by the previous administration, and an estimated 70 percent turned over in the administration before that. Secretaries were told that they would not receive pay raises unless they joined the mayor's political party. Why was this not the source of outraged public complaint? The simple reason is that any idea of career paths had broken down. As one secretary put it: "For four years we've lived with controlled minds and closed mouths. If anyone would make a complaint [about illicit activities], he would lose his job. But everyone would comment to each other privately about what was going on."

Moreover, the internal systems for investigating complaints and for auditing had become victims of influence and incompetence. The accounts and records were now virtually useless, according to a team of experts working on the integrated system of financial management—which, by the way, still had not been put into place after four years. Though the design had not been completed entirely, another reason for the delay in implementing the new system was (in the words of the program's managers) "resistance by city employees who do not for their own reasons wish to be part of a system of financial management."

There was also centralized corruption. "The previous mayor set up an office called OPCC, the Office of Planning, Coordination, and Control," related the new director of this office. "OPCC centralized everything, every decision. At the end every permit and every license and every contract had to be approved there. This became the source of much abuse. We've nicknamed it the Office of Planning and Collection of *Coimas* [bribes]."

In some ways the situation was better than in 1985. Some of the reforms undertaken then had stuck. The deregulation of some areas of the city economy permanently removed the corruption that formerly attended the enforcement of those regulations. Cutting back the role of the city government in other ways also helped. For example, the city had not returned to being a major construction company, although its stock of equipment had been enlarged through a foreign aid project. But unfortunately the process of selecting and supervising public works projects had deteriorated, and major forms of corruption had emerged again.

In a poll of Paceños in February 1996, 50 percent of the population agreed that "the level of corruption with respect to the past is worse." Another 43 percent said it was the same. No one said it was better—the other 7 percent said "don't know." (The poll was referring to all levels of government, not just the city.) Some 74 percent of the respondents said that Bolivian politicians are less honest than those in other parts of Latin America. When asked whether the primary motive of politicians was public service, "economic ambition," or "ambition for power," 84 percent of male respondents and 52 percent of females said "economic ambition." Only 9 percent of the combined sample said "public service."[1]

Not surprisingly, the mismanagement and corruption in La Paz were accompanied by an alarming trend in city finances. Mayor MacLean-Abaroa's last full year in office was 1990 (under Bolivian law he had to resign about halfway through 1991, in order to become a candidate for reelection at the end of that year). From 1990 to 1995, the deficit of expenditures over current income (excluding capital transfers and foreign aid) rose from approximately US$1.2 million (4 percent of current income) to about US$40.7 million (87 percent of current income). Over the same period and again using current dollars, total investment moved from US$10.4 million to US$14.6 million, whereas current expenditures grew much faster, from US$8.5 million to US$32.0 million in 1995.

What had gone wrong? And what could be done now to deal with the problems?

INFORMATION AND INCENTIVES

The La Paz case demonstrates two lessons. First, a significant dent can be made in systematic corruption. Second, over time and under new leadership, some of the anti-corruption measures may become distorted and actually turn into sources of other forms of corruption. This raises a host of questions. Why is there backsliding? What are the implications for designing anti-corruption policies?

The first point to notice is that La Paz is not alone. Other cities, and other countries, have had difficulty in sustaining anti-corruption initiatives. Hong Kong's example is instructive. The anticipation of 1997 had a big impact. In the words of one report, "Uncertainty about Hong Kong's future after China takes over next July is fueling an urge to get rich quick."[2] Hong Kong's

Independent Commission against Corruption said that reports of corruption in the public and private sectors rose 58 percent from 1992 to 1994. (Reports of corruption then declined 10 percent in 1995.) Agents at Kroll Associates (Asia), a leading international consultancy, say that its caseload of white-collar crime has doubled from January 1995 to June 1996. Kroll's managing director, Stephen Vickers, complains that neither the police nor the ICAC has brought high-profile corporate investigations to trial in the past two years.

The problem is that China is widely perceived to be the most corrupt country in Asia. It garnered this dubious honor in a ranking published by Transparency International in May 1996, based on a number of commercial rating services. Hong Kong then ranked close to the other end of the scale. People are worried that well-connected Chinese companies operating in Hong Kong are bringing in corrupt habits, and that the rules of the game will change in this and other ways.

Sustaining policies across administrations is difficult in many areas of city government, not only in anti-corruption efforts. According to one recent, pessimistic review, very few cities in developing countries seem able to maintain short-term success along any dimension. Success stories such as "Curitiba, the Indian city of Bangalore, and a few other examples may indicate that the real problem facing poorer cities is not so much population growth or their resource base but a lack of competent leadership and sound regulations and policies that last beyond one administration."[3] Beyond a lack of leadership, Linden blames the problems for being, in general, too difficult for cities in developing countries—migration, poverty, ecological setbacks, highly mobile international investment, stagnant food production, and rising crime and civil strife.

Is this also true of corruption? Is it simply too hard to overcome in a sustainable way?

The first point is that city governments will remain relatively lucrative, relatively vulnerable targets for the unscrupulous. Compared with national governments, municipal administrative systems are usually weaker. Pay scales for professionals are lower, leading to lower-quality personnel on average. Because of scale effects, the possibilities for co-optation by local élites or local populists seem higher. For better or worse, cities in many countries are the most accessible form of state power and wealth. In the hands of unscrupulous opportunists or idealists unable to manage, city governments can easily become the sites of petty tyrannies or systematic corruption or both. The threats are endemic.

An economic approach to corruption asks that we focus on activities where the unscrupulous can create monopoly rents, use official discretion for personal gain, and avoid accountability. Getting the government out of (monopoly) businesses in which (competitive) firms can provide the service is one useful idea. Taking into account the possible corruption of any regulation may well lead to deregulating, to an extent greater than would be optimal in a perfectly functioning state. On the other hand, privatizing and deregulating carry their own risks of corruption, inefficiency, and injustice. The very act of privatization can itself be corrupted, as recent experience in many countries sadly shows. Deregulation is fine if the regulations have no social benefits; but in environments characterized by thin markets, cartels, poor information, and high uncertainty, a deregulated market may itself be subject to massive inefficiencies and injustice.

We have seen that inspired city leaders can create effective strategies against systematic corruption that work in the short term. For example, they can change information and incentives in such a way that monopoly rents are reduced. But in the longer term, when leadership changes, it is always possible that anti-corruption efforts can be disassembled. The single registry of all transactions was dismantled in La Paz, and plans for an integrated financial management system have still not borne fruit. Taxpayers undermined the "auto-evaluation" of their properties, and the lack of systematic record keeping made it impossible for the authorities to check records over time. (Tax officials may well have preferred to keep things disorganized, so they could extort bribes from individuals in exchange for lower tax payments.) Meritocratic hiring and promotion practices were subverted by mayors who wanted to use top city jobs as patronage.

Not only can anti-corruption measures be dismantled, they can also themselves become corrupted. In La Paz, increasing the salaries of officials in key technical positions was an important step in turning the city around. But by 1991 it had become the source of political controversy and a campaign issue (as in many cases when people make a decent living in government). Then, after the change of mayors, it became the vehicle for installing friends and members of the political party in power in top jobs for which they were technically unqualified. The idea of combining privatization with strict regulation can be corrupted first by subverting the bidding and awarding processes and then by invalidating the supervision and quality control functions of government. A centralized system for managing all procurement can, of course, become its own corrupt monopoly.

The forces of democratic elections and economic competition do provide some checks on corruption. Local tyrannies are constrained by the democratic process, even when populist and redistribution issues take center stage. A competitive economy will tend to overthrow cartels and collusive arrangements, at least if minimal efforts are made at providing transparency in government-business relationships. And yet, as ancient and modern philosophers have described, democracy is no guarantee against corruption.[4]

The long-term solutions to retrogression would seem to lie in creating structures of self-interest that build on democratic and free-market principles. To the extent that citizens who are victims of corruption can gain more access to, control over, and feedback to corrupted systems, then the existence of illicit activities should become more evident and the prospects for sustainable reform more promising. The business community in the broadest sense has an interest both in efficient city services and in competitive provision of goods and services in general. Naturally, the temptation will arise for free riders to profit by providing a less valuable service or evading taxes or securing a monopoly through a bribe. But if collective action by businesspeople can be encouraged, perhaps sometimes with help from the public sector as through the enforcement of advertising laws or quality standards or competitive behavior, then in the long run their collective interest should tend to control corruption.

Incentive structures within the city government are also crucial. One may anticipate that leaders of corrupt city governments, and more generally corrupt companies, nongovernment organizations, and universities, will have a greater interest in cleaning up corruption in the revenue area than elsewhere. This, indeed, seems to have been the case in La Paz. City revenues have risen, nowhere more than in the revenues raised by the city itself (as opposed to transfers from the federal government of a share of taxes raised in La Paz and nationally), such as (since 1993) property taxes and taxes on vehicles. Here even an otherwise slack and corrupt administration may install a high-quality director and provide him or her with resources and support.

The incentives facing bureaucrats are also important determinants of corruption. Mayor MacLean-Abaroa did undertake some pay-for-performance experiments, but these efforts were not institutionalized. The city did not institute more general systems of performance-based pay and promotion within the municipal government. The merit system proved easy for the subsequent administrations to undermine. This suggests that a sustainable strategy will involve performance-based pay in which the public has much greater knowledge of and interest in maintaining performance and avoiding corruption. Fees for services and voucher-style ideas are interesting options, as is the greater decentralization of city services. In general, the more the public is involved in measuring the performance of city government and the more its evaluations are listened to and transformed into financial incentives, the more resistant a city government should be to corruption and abuse. This participation requires reforms in both information and incentives.

1. The information that is needed concerns the results of city activities and employees' efforts, both in terms of positive outcomes and negative ones such as corruption.
2. The incentives are an employee's and an office's rewards and punishments and how these are linked with information about results.

In La Paz there was almost no credible information about public works, tax collection, the granting of permits and licenses, the efficiency of procurement, and the abuse of office. Incentive systems have therefore easily been subverted by favoritism. A remedial strategy must address these systematic shortcomings.

How might such feedback and performance indicators be facilitated? Many of the important factors will go beyond the confines of municipal government. There are analogies to transactions costs and information costs, which may be reduced by better education systems, freer press, better legal systems, better communications infrastructure, and the like. Other things being equal, we should expect more client feedback the more advanced are these facilitating mechanisms.[5]

It is therefore possible to adopt an economic perspective on corruption and explain the retrogression in terms of monopoly powers, weak information systems, and incentive systems that are easily undermined by the unscrupulous. For reasons economists can understand, the avaricious side of human nature finds a particularly hospitable environment, noble exceptions aside, in settings characterized by poverty, instability, and social disintegration.

The story is of course not exclusively economic. Good leadership and competent employees make a difference. To put it another way, even good systems can be subverted. Many citizens in Hong Kong are worried that the remarkable powers of the Independent Commission against Corruption may be misused after the transition to Chinese sovereignty. As experience in many countries shows, the best of legal systems and organization charts may fail if employees are incompetent and unmotivated.

Leaders change, for worse as well as better; and political and other forces can lead to the replacement of competent employees by those who, even if willing, are unable to manage systems of information, control, and incentives. There is no once-and-for-all cure for corruption. But we can make our anti-corruption efforts more sustainable:

- the more competitive we can make the supply of goods and services;
- the simpler and less encumbering we can make regulations and permits;

- the more efficient is citizens' feedback about the good and bad things government does;
- the more closely we can link this feedback to the monetary and nonmonetary rewards of city officials; and
- the more transparent are municipal affairs.

It should be no surprise by this point in the book to notice that these are also good guidelines for a more efficient and just city administration.

Appendix: Corruption in Procurement

When a municipality needs a good or service, the city government has the two broad alternatives of *making it or buying it*: that is, the city can provide the good or service itself, or procure it from the private sector. Corruption is one of the dimensions of this choice. Much of this book concerns corruption that occurs when a city *provides* a service. This appendix concentrates on situations in which a municipality has decided to *procure* from the private sector, examines the kinds of corruption that may arise, and discusses potential countermeasures. It is probably the area of municipal corruption where the most money is involved. Because contracting is "where the money is"—to quote Willie Sutton on why he robbed banks—procurement is an area in which corruption is always a threat.

Among the principal types are collusion in bidding (leading to higher costs/prices for the city, payments for which may or may not be shared with corrupt officials); kickbacks by firms to "fix" procurement competition; and bribes to officials who regulate the winning contractor's behavior (which may permit lowball bids with subsequent cost overruns and unnecessary changes in contract specifications).

Procurement contracting often entails large monetary sums and involves widely known or powerful people inside and outside government. Thus, this kind of corruption can be especially damaging to a municipality in terms of distorted incentives, undermined public trust, and inequitable distribution of wealth and power.

The C = M + D − A formula offers a sound baseline for understanding the propensity toward corruption during each phase of a procurement. The ideal of "low" M, "low" D, and "high" A helps illuminate each step, along with the realization that under some circumstances the costs of achieving this ideal in terms of delays, quality, administrative overhead, and lost opportunities may simply be too high. For example, a central choice in every procurement is whether a custom product is required or an off-the-shelf product is adequate, with the efficiency gains of procuring the custom-designed product being balanced against likely increases in price and avoiding the hidden costs of corruption (which may be large) associated with procuring the "standard" item.

Recent work in economics and public policy suggests new twists to the analysis of procurement efficiency and corruption. For example, as we shall see, some important work calls for more rather than less discretion by procurement officials. In other circumstances studied by theorists, some collusion may be good, because it can help firms overcome tremendous uncertainty about the true costs of a project, thereby helping them avoid suicidally low bids. One qualitative lesson is that there are inevitable trade-offs in procurement, and here as elsewhere in public management, fighting corruption is not the sole aim.

Box A1: Procurement and corruption: A Framework for government officials

STYLIZED PROCUREMENT PROCESS	A. TYPES OF CORRUPTION AND PROBLEMS	B. CONDITIONS MOST CONDUCIVE TO CORRUPTION	C. INDICATORS OF POTENTIAL CORRUPTION	D. CONVENTIONAL POLICY REMEDIES TO STEM OR PREVENT CORRUPTION
STEP 1 Government establishes and publicizes need for a good or service.	*A1* Overspecification Lock-out specifications	*B1* Government cannot specify needs well high-tech/leading-edge projects mediocre public servants Poor career system, pay, compensation	*C1* Vague or nonexistent specifications Particular brand or function for equipment mandated "Emergency" need/contract Vendor helped establish specifications	*D1* Elevate procurement authority to high level (presumably to a talented person of high integrity) Use outside consultants to help establish requirements and explore the possibility frontier
STEP 2 Vendors submit proposals to meet the need.	*A2* Collusion/bid-rigging cover bidding bid suppression bid rotation market division (e.g., along regional lines)	*B2* Price- or quality-only competition Inelastic government demand Bids and identities of vendors announced publicly Firms homogeneous, have opportunities for frequent communication Government procurement agent has wide discretion	*C2* Number of firms small or market share constant over time Patterns develop over time Information that bids are greater than market-clearing prices Consistent vendor "fingerprints" on all bids	*D2* Promote additional competition Select bidders Change the rewards and penalties facing bidders Use information to raise likelihood of detecting and punishing collusion Restructure procurer-bidder relationship Change attitudes/culture
STEP 3 Government evaluates vendors' proposals and selects winner.	*A3* Bureaucratic corruption bribes kickbacks political considerations (pork barrel) Principal-agent mismatch cost or quality focus firm-specific favoritism mismatch in agent's incentives and risks	*B3* Large contracts (relative to markets) Overregulated and by-the-numbers procurement environment Quality (or cost) is the single measure of merit for awarding the contract	*C3* Contract awarded to other than low bidder Contract awarded to vendor with no track record Sole-source (no bid) Contract is rebid Government statement of work modified after initial need promulgated Overinvoicing	*D3* Elevate procurement authority to high level Increase penalties Increase transparency of proposal evaluation and vendor selection (written justifications, bid openings in public, outside reviews) Announce random "sting" operations
STEP 4 Vendor performs contract.	*A4* *Ex-post* corruption (excessive rents) fraudulent (inflated) cost reporting faulty overhead (cross-subsidization)	*B4* Sole-source situation Vendor in many markets, public and private sector	*C4* Cost overruns Sole-source extensions Award cancellation Poor quality Multiple change orders Protracted production or delivery schedule	*D4* Rotate agents Require periodic competition for routine procurements Dedicate additional resources (e.g., agents) to oversight activities Use market/cost surveys

A STYLIZED FOUR-STEP PROCUREMENT PROCESS

Procurement begins when the government establishes a need for a good or service and solicits vendors to perform the work or deliver the services. This statement of need step of a procurement is known also as the "Request for Proposals" or "Invitation for Bids" stage. In the second step, interested vendors submit bids. The government agency evaluates the vendors' proposals, selects a winner, and negotiates a contract in step three. In step four, the vendor performs the contract. Box A1 depicts these stages, with an italicized letter and number combination identifying each cell (from *A1* through *D4*).

Let us work our way column by column through this somewhat daunting table. In the paragraphs that follow, labels in bold italics (for example, ***[Cell C2]***) refer to the corresponding cells in the table. Our objective is to understand the kinds of corruption that may emerge at each step and to consider countermeasures and their costs.

TYPES OF CORRUPTION THAT CHARACTERIZE EACH STEP

[Cell A1] Early on, it is in a vendor's interest to influence the statement of need to emphasize the vendor's strengths and de-emphasize its weaknesses, thus biasing the competition. Opportunities for this may occur during routine exchanges of information with the government before the statement of need is published, especially in situations involving highly technical specifications that are better understood by the contractor than by the government. Also, city officials may corruptly share inside information that gives certain bidders an unfair advantage. Another possibility is "overspecification," where—possibly in exchange for a bribe—the procurement official excludes vendors by virtue of overly differentiated products or by the sheer weight and breadth of the requirements. A "lock-out" specification is one that excludes all but one bidder.

[Cell A2] During step two, a cartel of vendors can collude, or rig bids, to ensure that one of its number wins the contract. Canada's Bureau of Competition Policy distinguishes four categories of bid-rigging.

1. **Cover bidding:** Firms submit token bids, usually too high, designed to ensure that a previously-selected cartel member wins the contract.
2. **Bid suppression:** Firms refrain from bidding or eliminate themselves from the competition to leave a clear path for the preselected supplier.
3. **Bid rotation:** Firms rotate winning bids among themselves and, through side payments, ensure each receives a "fair" share of business over time.
4. **Market division:** Firms divide the market along regional, product-unique, or other lines and refrain from competing beyond the designated boundaries.

Collusion may not involve bribing a government official. It can be a form of cartel behavior or anti-competitive activity that is illegal but not, strictly speaking, corrupt. On the other hand, bid-rigging rings often do have the resources and sometimes the force to bribe or threaten government officials who would expose them.

[Cell A3] The evaluation process, the third step, may give rise to bribes and kickbacks, in return for favorable consideration of a vendor's bid, and to "pork-barrel" politics, in which politicians support bids that favor their constituencies or contributors. What might be called "mismatches" in the principal-agent relationship[1] may lead to inefficiency as well as collusion. Many of the indicators may be the same, and at times it may be difficult to differentiate the merely inefficient from the venal. Municipal leaders must be attuned to both.

[Cell A4] Corruption here can involve fraudulent (inflated) cost reporting, specifications changes, or faulty overhead claims. It may be easier for the larger companies, with many divisions and opportunities for cross-subsidizing work, to effect corrupt activities at this stage. Note that possibilities for corruption at this stage affect the propensity to corrupt behavior during steps one and two. For example, corrupt vendors can "lowball" the initial bid to win the contract if inflated costs during contract performance are easy to claim or have been rigged in advance. Another form of corruption involves lower-than-promised quality, where inspectors or regulators are bribed not to notice.

CONDITIONS MOST CONDUCIVE TO CORRUPTION

[Cell B1] Municipalities are sometimes ill-equipped to specify their needs. Especially in areas of leading-edge technology, it is not unusual to find that vendors rather than civil servants have better knowledge of and insight into government needs. Nor will mediocre government procurement officials be capable of articulating needs knowledgeably. In either case, the door is left open to corruption that preordains the winning contractor.

Should specifications be exact or flexible? There is no absolute answer, and problems can arise in either case. On the one hand, excessively vague specifications may prompt bids from vendors who are incapable of performing the work; on the other hand, more detailed and narrowly drawn specifications reduce the number of contractors who will be capable of submitting realistic bids. In the former case, administrative costs soar in the evaluation process and perhaps in the event that the product or service does not perform as required. In the latter, competition is limited. In either case, there are opportunities for corruption. Tight specifications limit discretion but may also enhance monopoly power among vendors. The net effects on efficiency and corruption will vary from case to case.

[Cell B2] At step two, the C = M + D − A formula offers a sound guideline. Anything that confers monopolistic advantages makes corruption more likely. Similarly, the likelihood for corruption will increase when official discretion is high and accountability is low, such as in a procurement based only on subjective measures of quality. In some cases, a monopolistic arrangement and high discretion are warranted, as we shall see. But the risks of inefficiency and corruption must be borne in mind.

[Cell B3] In the evaluation step, large (monetary) contracts relative to the market size offer corrupt actors additional wiggle room in which to hide illicit amounts. Discretion is obviously a problem. But there is a trade-off here between offering procurement agents additional discretion to make judgment calls to settle vague or hard-to-define specification evaluations on the one hand—which opens the possibility for corruption—and overly constraining the discretion of the procuring agent with rules and regulations to govern every decision on the other. (We shall return to this trade-off, which depends on the commodity or service in question and on the environment of corruption in which the procurement process is embedded, later.)

[Cell B4] In sole-source situations, competition suffers and one-on-one relationships develop over time. Cost-plus contracts may offer tempting opportunities for vendors to "goldplate"

products, adding luxuries and qualities beyond the original understanding. In addition, when vendors are large and in many different business lines, corrupt managers can mask cross-subsidization and fraudulent overhead charges more easily. In general, regulators will be more susceptible to bribes the vaguer are the criteria for cost overruns and the less clear is their own accountability.

INDICATORS OF POTENTIALLY CORRUPT ACTIVITY

Detecting corrupt procurement operations is frequently complicated because inefficiency and corruption are difficult to differentiate. None of the indicators that follow is by itself a sure sign of corruption in a particular case. As a consequence, these indicators are only guidelines for suggesting where detailed investigation may be warranted.

[Cell C1] In the need establishment step, any action that deviates from the standard pace and practice of procurements may indicate illicit activities. Possible indicators include: vague or nonexistent specifications; requests for specific brands or equipment that must perform in a narrowly defined area (overly restrictive specifications); "eleventh-hour" emergencies; or evidence that vendors have been unusually active in defining the municipality's needs.

[Cell C2] Several indicators have proven useful in signaling collusion in the bid submission step. Inexplicable patterns in bidding can emerge. For example, the number of firms bidding on contracts of a particular type or in a particular region remains small or constant over time, despite many potential competitors; public sector market shares held by single firms or groups of firms among a larger number of competitors stay constant; information from auditors and investigators reveals bids using prices that differ substantially from imputed or real market prices; the handwriting or writing style of a specific vendor appears on all submitted bids. Any of these could indicate the presence of bid-rigging. Several of them occurring at the same time may warrant a detailed investigation.

[Cell C3] Many events can signal the possibility of corruption during the vendor selection step of the procurement process. For example, a contract is awarded to a vendor who did not submit the lowest bid or to one who has no prior experience in the contract's substantive area. The contract is awarded through a rebid. A bid or contract is designated as sole-source. Modifications are made to the government statement of work that trigger a reopening of the entire procurement process. Again, none of these is a sure sign. A consistent pattern of such events, though, is a sign of a procurement process that is not as efficient as it could be.

[Cell C4] In the delivery stage of a contract, a number of indicators are correlated with corruption and inefficiency, though none is a necessary or sufficient condition. The contract experiences unexpected cost overruns—for example, beyond those explained in terms of inflation or an altered specification. The contract experiences important or numerous change orders. Extensions of the contract are granted on a sole-source basis. An award is cancelled. The products or services do not perform as specified. The schedules of production or delivery are protracted. Costs that are significantly higher than national or international benchmarks may also indicate illicit activities.

POLICY REMEDIES

Remedies to systematic corruption in procurement are many. Succeeding in the fight to prevent corruption requires leaders to make an unequivocal commitment to break from the "business as usual" and "go along to get along" mindsets and to dedicate government resources to fighting corruption. That said, leaders must always be aware of the costs entailed in any anti-corruption measure.

Before considering specific steps, two important conditions that help battle corruption in the procurement arena should be mentioned. First, a well-delineated civil service career system is fundamental. Municipal leaders must ensure that government officials are paid decent wages, are promoted on merit, and have clearly defined career paths. Second, mayors must work closely with investigative and law enforcement agencies outside the municipality. Crucial mistakes can be avoided if information is shared from the beginning of a suspected case of fraud or collusion. Obviously, the chances of succeeding in the fight against corruption are enhanced if these agencies are talented and honest.

Other general conditions favor the fight against corruption, such as the presence of democratic institutions, a free and aggressive press, and societal norms promoting honesty. Statistical work across countries shows that when investors rate a country's level of corruption high, the country also tends to have poor economic and political rights, high levels of regulation and state involvement in the economy, political and economic instability, and low levels of economic growth.[2]

Most of these conditions are of course beyond the control of municipal leaders. They may nonetheless reduce the scope for corruption in procurement by following the logic of the C = M + D − A formula. For example:

Promote competitive conditions where feasible. Encouraging competitive environments in areas where monopolies (other than "natural" monopolies) might otherwise emerge will eliminate

Box A2: When the Competitive Model Breaks Down

The competitive model posits a situation in which large numbers of qualified vendors will answer the call for proposals to satisfy government (or private sector) needs, and a discriminating and value-maximizing authority selects the vendor who can provide the goods and services at the lowest price possible, thus maximizing the public good. At the limit in the classical economic model, prices for goods are set at the marginal cost of producing them. Unfortunately, reality deviates substantially from the ideal; and the purely competitive model that guarantees equity, honesty, and efficiency can break down in several possible ways, including:

1. Uncertainty in information available to procurement officials renders the competitive model ineffective in ensuring against corruption in some cases (and it may be inefficient to boot).
2. The government at times does not know well what it needs, especially on highly technical projects in which the benefits of specialization are significant (for example, information systems areas).
3. Procurements requiring highly differentiated products with unique design features or that may press the technology frontier may not bring forth more than a handful of, and in many cases only one or two, bidders.
4. The public's opportunity cost losses from "competition by fiat" may be large, because vendors may not make certain optional contract-specific investments which they would make were past experience more acceptable as a criterion for winning future contracts and because vendors have no incentive to share wisdom and expertise in developing needs. (Kelman states these points elegantly.[a])
5. Contractors may be risk averse, especially on very large projects, prompting government to share in the risks and introducing moral hazards into the procurement process.
6. Defining the "public good" and translating it into contractually enforceable terms are difficult to accomplish. In addition, the procurement officials charged with procuring goods at socially efficient prices sometimes do not share the public's preferences and trade-offs (the principal-agent problem).

Some observers have seized on these and other inadequacies of the "fair and open" competition model and proposed alternatives. They seek ways to capture the benefits attendant to longer-term relationships, to move beyond "by-the-book" procurements, and to create incentives for rewarding past performance. Kelman recommends among other things that more discretion be accorded procuring officials and that past performance not be excluded from the vendor selection process.[b]

Notes: a. Kelman, *Procurement and Public Management.*
b. Kelman, *Procurement and Public Management.*

some opportunities for corrupt behavior. The operative theory is that many qualified vendors eager for work will compete for business, which will be won by the most efficient supplier, thus driving the cost of the procurement down and securing the greatest value (surplus) for the public. The purchaser (the city government) may also easily threaten to use an alternative supplier. Both theory and some empirical evidence show that competitive, nonintegrated industries tend to favor arms-length procurement and carefully specified contracts.[3]

One method of promoting competition might be to divide large projects into smaller ones to expand the number of potential competitors beyond vendors that are large or that have excess capacity. This tactic is especially useful on purchases that are large in volume or that deal with products for which costs and quality are well understood.

As we shall see below, the competitive model breaks down in some well-known ways, due to information asymmetries, highly differentiated or technically sophisticated needs, principal-agent mismatches, and others (described in Box A2). But as a starting point for any municipal effort to enhance efficiency and fight corruption, it is good to prefer and if possible engender more rather than less competition.

Simplify and clarify rules and regulations. When corruption becomes an issue, it is almost a reflex to think of new rules and laws as the solution. The idea is to reduce arbitrary discretion, promote competition, and protect fairness and efficiency by standardizing procedures so they are transparent and so deviations from the norm are easy to detect.

This strategy often backfires. True, the immediate costs of issuing new rules may seem small. Politicians may believe that this sort of "getting tough" generates political benefits, and promoting new rules and layers of oversight may seem to politicians to be a good form of insurance in case further corruption scandals erupt. But in many cases, the new rules and oversight create large costs. The attendant administrative load can be heavy. Moreover, imposing new rules without careful analysis may actually restrict competition and give officials new monopoly powers with which to exact bribes.

A regulation can create or reduce opportunities for corruption. A good rule of thumb is this. If a regulation creates a new monopoly power, such as a new regulator; if it creates new discretion in determining its applicability, timing, or effects; and if it makes it more difficult for citizens, bidders, and other parts of government to know what is happening, then the regulation will tend to augment corruption rather than reduce it.

But if a regulation makes it easier for suppliers or parts of government to compete; if it paints "brighter lines" with less room for subjective judgments; and if it enhances accountability by making possible new indicators of performance and malfeasance, then corruption will tend to diminish. And—we quickly add—the efficiency of city operations will tend to improve.

Strengthen accountability and transparency through the three oversight mechanisms of auditing, inspecting, and investigating. Modern auditing and financial systems, self-policing by the private sector, inspection and investigative techniques, and computer-assisted analysis (perhaps confidential diagnostics) can create institutional change by assigning responsibilities accurately, detecting patterns of illicit behavior early, and introducing transparency. In addition, these initiatives deter corruption.

Finding the appropriate balance between rules and regulations on the one hand and discretion on the other is a consideration in situations where corruption exists but not in epidemic proportions. The former confer predictability and legitimacy on the procurement system; the latter offers opportunities for honest, entrepreneurial-minded public servants to achieve excellence. Changing the underlying systemic structure—which often means transforming the principal-agent relationship with results-driven incentive systems—is at the heart of this guideline and is discussed at length later, in the section on recent initiatives.

Several pieces of specific advice are relevant at each stage of the procurement process. The municipal leader can use the cells in Box A1 to develop a first cut at policy analysis and remedies. After assessing the types, conditions, and indicators of potential corruption in the city, a leader can look to Column D for a menu of policy initiatives that may be appropriate for detailed consideration.

[Cell D1] To guard against corruption in step one, the government should ensure that top-quality people serve in procurement positions. One approach is to elevate procurement authority to a sufficiently high level in the management hierarchy that experienced and honest officials control procurement. But the nuts and bolts of everyday procurement activities will require able public servants at the lower levels, freeing higher-level managers to focus on the overall system and removing them from the grinding details of procurement contracts. In the United States, procurement reforms instituted by the Department of Defense since the mid-1980s have included strict education and experience standards for all officials who serve in procurement-designated positions. But in many municipalities around the world, procurement officials are untrained and poorly paid. Sometimes they are appointed for political reasons, in order to reap the benefits of kickbacks for the political party in power. Whether through faulty structures and incentives or through active design by municipal politicians, unprofessional and poorly motivated procurement officials are at the heart of many corrupt cities.

A second approach is to bring in experts outside the procuring agency to help establish need requirements and fill gaps in technical knowledge that might otherwise permit an unethical vendor to exploit the agency. This approach might employ specialized procurement boards across municipal agencies or could entail privatizing the management and evaluation of procurement. Specialized agencies such as the Swiss Société Générale de Surveillance or British Crown Agents have experience in designing and implementing complicated procurement operations. Using such external agencies does not eliminate collusive temptations totally, but their extranational scope and the value to the parent company of a reputation for probity mean that the internal incentives are more likely to favor honesty.

[Cell D2] Combating collusive bidding is much studied, yet it remains a difficult problem to detect and deter. Box 6 refines this important cell in the procurement table in some detail.

Methods of selecting bidders include screening for past performance,[4] determining honesty and financial wherewithal; using outside guarantees of honest bids and faithful performance; and in cases where the competitive model breaks down, selecting a single firm and negotiating "ruthlessly" with it.[5] Note that, in general, the earlier in the procurement process a municipality takes steps to deal with likely corrupt vendors, the less exacting are the standards of proof required to disqualify firms. Litigation after the fact is expensive in time and money due to exacting rules of discovery and burden of proof requirements imposed on government. *Ex ante,* the government can in principle be nimbler, but there is always the trade-off with the possibility of arbitrary and even corrupt behavior. When discretion increases, it may be possible to move faster, but it also may be possible to use that power illicitly—see the following discussion on the possibility that prequalification may itself be corruptly misused.

Changing rewards and penalties facing bidders will alter their calculations. For example, incentive contracts can favor ethical (and efficient) bidders by tying monetary rewards or future contracts to costs and quality. Strengthening the severity and certainty of penalties, disbarment, criminal sanctions, and publicity will damage a transgressing company's reputation, and will therefore help deter a would-be bid-rigger.

Information strategies raise the likelihood of detecting collusion and thereby offer, in conjunction with strengthened penalties, a powerful deterrent. Four specific approaches include: Use computer systems to detect collusion by identifying patterns in bidding; increase the number of agents trained to do undercover work, surveillance, cost estimation, and market surveys; gain "inside" information from third parties (for example, industry newsletters, consultants, and auditors); and seek information from bidders themselves (disaffected employees, losing bidders, and nonbidders).

Restructuring the procurer-bidder relationship can increase competition by aggressively encouraging new firms to enter the bidding through publicity, risk-sharing, and wider publicity; reducing the discretionary authority of the procurement official through rules about change orders, sole-source follow-ons, and "emergency"-qualifying situations; rotating procurement officials to preclude cozy familiarity with contractors; redefining the organization's needs to make possible purchasing standardized goods with established market prices; integrating vertically to produce and provide the good publicly; and making "corruptibility" a criterion when establishing input specifications and measures of merit for performance. The core notion is to structure the relationship between municipality and vendors to replace the temptations for corruption with a set of rewards that penalize poor performance but reward both the procuring official and the contractor who create value (surplus) for the municipality.

Finally, the procuring authority can promote change in cultural attitudes about collusion by disassociating collusion from practices and goals deemed acceptable, educating contractors regarding the competitive bidding process, and promoting the bidders' identification with the social or public purpose of the contract.

[CELL D3] Combating corruption in step three of the procurement process can take many forms. Decision authority can be raised to a high level, presumably gaining the benefits of hierarchical reviews and the wisdom of a senior, and therefore visible, procurement official who may have more to lose than gain by engaging in favoritism. Increasing the severity and certainty of penalties to public officials (and their private sector counterparts) caught in illicit contracting schemes deters repeated offenses. The transparency of the evaluation can be enhanced in several ways: (1) requiring written justifications and top-level reviews for contract awards to other than the lowest bidder or in procurements with unusual actions like rebids, sole-source contracts, and altered statements of work; (2) opening bids in public; and (3) requiring an outside review of procurement decisions, as either a regular feature of each procurement or at random.

For deterrence purposes, municipal leaders could announce publicly a fixed number of random "sting" operations to be conducted over some fixed time period, say during a year. Although contract participants are well aware that such surveillance goes on regularly behind the scenes, announcing the certainty of some small number of resource-intensive stings gives the idea topical relevance and visibility. This would serve to give the unethical vendor or procurement official second thoughts about colluding, or at least raise the costs of doing so without detection.

[CELL D4] In step four, two standard techniques—rotating agents and allocating additional resources to investigations and surveillance—help deter as well as reduce opportunities for corruption. For routine procurements of standardized goods, contracts can be recommitted at regular time intervals. Market and cost surveys are useful when extending sole-source supplier contracts on a regular (perhaps annual) basis.

RECENT WORK ON PROCUREMENT

Elected officials, government policy makers, and academics continue to focus on ways to make the procurement process both more efficient and less vulnerable to corruption. For example, the policy and academic literature regarding the principal-agent problem and its emphasis on incentive-intensive contracts continues to expand. Modern developments range across all steps in the procurement process and are generally more applicable in municipalities that have talented civil servants, enjoy some of the advantages of democracy (especially a coherent legal system backed up by courts of law), and have made progress in breaking the "culture of impunity" in which corruption flourishes.

At the heart of these advances is recognition that the model of pure competition, however appropriate to delineate the boundaries of the environment in which procurement takes place and however desirable as an ideal, is sometimes inadequate in the real world. Asymmetries in information, unforeseen technology breakthroughs, unique innovations, and uncertain or hard-to-measure quality features make it difficult to argue that competitive bidding, unshared information, and perfectly specified contacts are either feasible or desirable.

One well-known example is "winner's ruin," where the winning firm loses money because it underestimates costs—and subsequently may underperform or default on the contract.[6] Under some circumstances, allowing bidders to share proprietary information about costs may lead to socially more optimal bids, but doing so obviously also facilitates collusion. Indeed, some economists have argued that, under some admittedly extreme circumstances, collusion may be preferable to independent bids.[7]

A second example concerns the so-called "hold-up problem." After winning the contract, the supplier develops considerable proprietary information that gives it an advantage in further contract bids. With this private information, the provider can use what is effectively monopoly power (now that it has won the contract) to increase charges. Dual-sourcing or cost-sharing arrangements may be effective responses; on the other hand, they can sacrifice economies of scale and specialization.

Let us now consider other examples where new insights enrich the discussion of efficiency and corruption in procurement. One mechanism that has broad applicability, especially at steps one and three of the procurement process, is a "protest" mechanism. Firms can file protests based on their belief that the statement of need unfairly excludes them or that the evaluation process was biased or otherwise inappropriate. This initiative vests a quasi-judicial board with authority to subpoena documents, discipline government officials, and reevaluate procurement decisions. The protests entail potentially lengthy delays and the administrative costs of filing, defending, and adjudicating. As such they can be costly to the procurement official, to the competing firms, and to the public. On the other hand, incentives for scrupulous behavior on the parts of government and vendors are therefore reinforced. Moreover, government can harness the self-interest of losing bidders and non-colluders who protest to detect and police corruption. A protest process is one of the central provisions of the Competition in Contracting Act passed by the U.S. Congress in 1984 to cover procurements of automated data processing and telecommunications equipment.[8]

A second valuable initiative is motivating procurement officials with incentives tied to contract performance. Though this idea is not new, tying pay to performance fell into benign disuse during the era of the entitlement mentality. The idea is undergoing a renaissance as public and private sector managers streamline and downsize with an emphasis on competition, meritocracy, and performance accountability—all of which require more extensive and better information gathering.[9] The "incentive intensity" principle of the principal-agent relationship can help municipal leaders and their procurement teams motivate procurement "agents" of the government and diminish the temptations for corrupt behavior at all steps of the procurement process, especially steps one, three, and four. The incentive intensity principle tells us that agents' incentives should be an increasing function of the marginal returns to the task, the accuracy with which performance can be measured, the responsiveness of the effort to incentives, and the agents' risk tolerance.[10] Taken against a backdrop of institutional reform that includes better information and worker participation, incentive-based pay is a potentially powerful tool for the municipal leader.[11]

The idea of prequalifying bidders on procurement contracts has undergone further development in recent years. This initiative extends the common idea of prescreening or preselecting bidders one step further by formalizing and publicizing the process, often through use of a questionnaire. To uncover potential irregularities, detailed reviews are conducted of a vendor's key people (reputations and affiliations with other companies within and external to the involved industry), company affiliations (for example, interlocking boards of directors), financial assets and liabilities, and prior experience.

Prequalification is the centerpiece of a set of administrative tools—used in conjunction with but outside the legal and law enforcement systems—in New York City's attack on corruption in school construction contracts. To help rein in the widespread corruption plaguing school construction, the New York City School Construction Authority's Office of the Inspector General now prequalifies—using a forty-page questionnaire—every firm that hopes to be considered for school construction contracts. Its efficacy is reflected in the comment: "A number of firms have made clear that they fear the administrative sanction of a disbarment far more than a criminal prosecution." Over five years, the process coupled with other administrative sanctions has worked well in breaking the back of corruption.[12]

The extensive procurement activity of government at all levels, coupled with the costs of oversight, makes it impossible to conduct detailed investigations of possible corrupt behavior in every project. But extraordinary technical advances in computers now make possible automated auditing and econometric analysis on a scale and at levels heretofore impossible. With decision rules based on information gleaned from investigations into corruption over time, models are quite accurate in "red-flagging" cases for possible irregularities. Bid-rigging in highway construction, for example, is indicated by an econometric model that compares bidding patterns of cartel and noncartel members.[13]

Applicable primarily in the evaluation and selection stage of the procurement process are the aforementioned protest mechanism, life-cycle criteria, independent evaluations (which build on the conventional idea), "revolving door" legislation, and the incentive intensity of the principal-agent relationship. To eliminate low buy-ins and the propensity for subsequent inflated costs, some procurements may use criteria based on a product's entire life cycle, from cradle to grave. Evaluation panels, in which consensus rules, can help preclude temptations for individuals to succumb to bribes, or render the bribes less effective if they occur. Outside consultants of impeccable integrity can conduct proposal reviews and select winners, removing the possibility of corruption on the part of the agent (though opening up obvious channels for the same kinds of corruption in different places). Some international organizations such as the aforementioned Swiss Société Générale de Surveillance and the British Crown Agents have managed procurement operations for governments and companies around the world. "Revolving door" legislation makes it more difficult for government employees to secure employment with companies with which they have established a relationship during several procurement engagements over time. Finally, the incentive intensity of the principal-agent relationship can both improve efficiency and reduce the propensity for need-driven corruption.

Several new approaches show promise to improve procurement during the delivery stage of the procurement process. In high-tech areas, such as computers, technology advances and learning curve improvements can drive costs down quickly, and the government can capture some of the benefits of these advances through "refreshment clauses." These clauses must be crafted to protect against technology obsolescence and exploitation by vendors who would otherwise extract the rents associated with the technology advance or learning curve effect. In effect, the clauses permit vendors to offer later-generation equipment that meets or exceeds the specifications of the originally-bid equipment at prices no higher than the original bid.

Dual-sourcing, sometimes used by the U.S. Department of Defense in high-tech weapons systems buys, is designed to prevent monopoly or sole-source rents *ex post* through an initial "educational" or "learning" buy of technology, which later may be transferred to a second vendor in a competitive bid. If sole-source contracts are used, market surveys for cost and quality as well as detailed accounts of a firm's actual costs can help establish prices and compensation for follow-ons. The U.S. Navy and Air Force have used this latter technique effectively in procuring jet engines for high performance aircraft from two suppliers, General Electric and Pratt and Whitney. Municipal leaders should consider dual-sourcing when goods are relatively resistant to obsolescing, when the products are within the known technology frontier, and when procurement contracts can be awarded for multiple years.[14]

Another idea—really building on and updating an older idea for modern times—with particular relevance to all steps of the procurement process is using external audit/oversight authorities. Simply put, in many situations internal auditors are not as credible or aggressive as external ones. Using external oversight was a key recommendation of the committee that recently examined corruption in the New York City Police Department, and is applicable to procurement policies at subnational levels. Already practiced at the national level in some countries (the United States and Great Britain, for example, have long used independent investigative and oversight bodies), the idea is built on keeping oversight independent by maintaining accountability in the functional area.[15]

As discussed in the text, citizens' groups and the private sector can help provide a kind of external oversight, recognizing the value in promoting fair competition and conducting business under conditions of probity. (Transparency International is one such example). Mayors should consider the many ways that bidders themselves might be induced to reveal corrupt practices and monitor themselves.

SECOND-ORDER EFFECTS

Many of these corruption-preventing countermeasures not only entail direct costs but "second-order" effects: changes prompted by the countermeasures themselves or dynamic consequences of unscrupulous players in the contracting process looking for workarounds to the newly imposed mode of conducting business. Some of the effects include opening the door to other kinds of corruption, and some merely make the procurement process inefficient and more costly to the public. Even the most straightforward tool, promulgating rules and regulations, can trigger corruption and costs.

First, rules may create opportunities for other types of corruption. For example, Gyawali notes that a typical pattern of corruption within Nepal's irrigation, sewage, and road construction public works projects "occurs within a structure of rules and regulations often so thick that it provides an ideal cover for profit skimming. Corruption is effected by meticulously observing the very rules designed to prevent corruption."[16]

Next, the administrative costs of new rules can be high, and efficiency can suffer. In addition, eliminating all but the most trivial discretionary decisions from the hands of procurement officials simultaneously restricts the opportunities for these same officials to achieve excellence in procurement by applying their expertise, common sense, and contract-specific knowledge. (This is a main argument in Steven Kelman's plea for discretion in procurement in computer systems in the United States.[17])

Promulgating additional rules and regulations should not therefore be an automatic response to corruption. When do rules and regulations help? The $C = M + D - A$ formula provides guidance. Rules tend to reduce corruption when they decrease monopoly power, clarify and limit discretion, and make accountability easier. They stimulate corruption when they grant officials new monopoly powers, with vague discretion and little transparency.

Many other anti-corruption initiatives exhibit the potential for these second-order effects. Using outside consultants, for example, removes public officials from the suspicion of collusion on contracts, but creates opportunities for collusion between the consultant and an unscrupulous vendor, or even between the consultant and the procurement official. Vertical integration, while perhaps unavoidable in some cases in which corruption is rife and the widely accepted cultural norm, puts the government in competition with the private sector for products the private sector can produce. This is the antithesis of competition, and it entails the standard "produce or buy" problem confronting many public officials. If government conducts surveillance on otherwise squeaky-clean firms, and is discovered doing so, damaging publicity could result. Risk-sharing contracts increase the likelihood of moral hazard—underinvestment by the contractor because part of its risk is "insured."[18] Rotating procurement agents through agencies or among functional areas has opportunity costs, especially denying the benefits of experience developed over time in specialized procurement areas. Cost surveys to establish the coming time period's payment schedule can encourage suppliers to inflate costs, or to use higher-cost methods, to ensure higher returns.

Nor are the more recent anti-corruption remedies without second-order problems. Here we consider the two examples of dual-sourcing and contract protests, discussing the latter in some depth.

Dual-Sourcing

Though dual-sourcing can work well in some cases, second-order problems crop up. First, because expected profits are lower from the beginning, some firms, perhaps even the most desirable ones, may choose not to compete, permitting higher-cost producers to bid and win the contract. Second, incentives for the winner of the "learning buy" contract to invest in research, development, and capital will be reduced, because expected future rents will be smaller. Though these second-order effects concern economic efficiency more than corruption *per se*, decreasing competition may open the door to collusion in the early stages. The winner of the first stage, to garner rents perhaps unavailable at a full-production second-stage buy, may be prompted to enter into collusive arrangements with competing vendors.

Similarly, prequalifying bidders for procurements can eliminate many prospective vendors who might otherwise be predisposed toward collusive activities. However, the prequalification process effectively shifts the possibilities for corruption back one step in the contracting process, creating another "chokepoint," entry to which must be regulated by some mechanism. As a consequence, the locus for corrupt activity may well become the process of qualifying for inclusion on the prequalification list. As Heymann observes: ". . . [O]verloading at any point in an administrative system requires a choice as to who can use it or in what order it shall be available to people, and this always creates discretion to decide who gets served at all and who gets served first. This discretionary power can be sold whether it is by an inspector who has to approve a new building or by an appointments secretary who controls access to a high-level official."[19]

Protest Mechanisms

Another example of a comparatively recent anti-corruption tool that may spawn undesirable second-order effects is the protest mechanism. In a system of well-recognized and enforceable laws and an empowered legal system, the protest mechanism in theory should enhance competition and help align procuring officials' incentives with decisions that optimize social value added. The mechanism deters corruption by giving its "victims"—high-quality vendors who lose bids for otherwise inexplicable reasons—a means to bring their legitimate complaints before a quasi-judicial body, and thereby help expose corruption. In effect, encouraging protests enhances transparency.

However, protests themselves come at some expense to the public good—directly, through the administrative and legal expenses of filing, defending against, and adjudicating the protest; and indirectly, through the opportunity costs associated with delaying needed construction or acquisitions unnecessarily. For contracts with very high value or with steep proposal preparation costs, especially those that will be performed over an extended time horizon, even vendors who lose for legitimate and appropriate reasons may be prompted to file protests as a matter of course. Even if this does not help the vendor defray a portion of the proposal costs through a protest settlement, it will signal to the company's top brass that the contract (and the work of those involved) was winnable had it not been for improprieties in the selection process. Indeed, Kelman reports: "About one-third of the most recently awarded major contracts that respondents discussed in the government Computer Managers Survey were protested."[20] A key contracting official at the U.S. Department of Agriculture notes, "Usually, when the low-price vendor doesn't win, there's a protest."[21]

Marshall et al. have defined the unintended side effects of the protest process in three categories:[22]

1. **Overdeterrence.** The government, through the procurement official, makes a non-optimal decision to avoid incurring the costs of a likely or threatened protest. A vendor's record of filing protests might confer legitimacy on the procurement official's decision, whether or not corruption was involved.
2. **"Fedmail."** Though a procurement official and process may have been beyond reproach in conducting a particular acquisition, the government may offer protesting companies cash payments to avoid legal expenses and time delays.
3. **Buy-offs.** Firms that have filed nonfrivolous protests settle on the side for cash payments from winning firms. Marshall et al. point out that the settlement process "provides colluding bidders with a marvelous legal forum in which to conduct their business—free communication is possible in conjunction with cash or in-kind side payments between seeming competitors."[23] In some cases, there may be little difference to the government between the price it pays under the settlement process and the price it would have paid had there been collusive bidding.[24]

Vendors will calculate the costs and benefits of filing a protest and presumably act rationally over many procurements. Calibrating the way the costs of the protest process are allocated (for example, using forfeitable bonds and assigning protest expenses to winning and losing protesters or government procurement agencies) may help bring the system into an equilibrium in which transparency and honesty are injected into the procurement system while social benefits are optimized.

Clearly, combating these effects is not straightforward. Of course, other initiatives instituted to deter corruption or to modify the system to eliminate inducements to corrupt behavior in the first place (that is, initiatives to decrease monopoly, establish incentives tied to desirable outcomes, and increase transparency) will serve to attenuate the incidence and severity of second-order corruption as well. Nonetheless, these dynamic effects are not entirely avoidable.

The point for municipal leaders to bear in mind is that breaking the culture of impunity created by systemic corruption in procurement requires strong medicine. Implementing a corruption-fighting strategy will involve applying a set of measures that, through second-order effects (and third-order, and so on), will create a new equilibrium in the procurement process. The hidden costs of these second-order effects can be large; and the municipal leader should at least be aware of their existence, if not guard explicitly against them, in tailoring a strategy of anti-corruption initiatives to city-unique characteristics.

CONCLUDING REMARKS

What, then, is a municipal leader interested in preventing corruption in procurement to do? The policy prescriptions can seem conflicting. For example, vague specifications may increase overhead costs by prompting an excessive number of bids, but tight specifications may elicit too few bids and make collusion easier. Permitting or forcing bidders to share proprietary information may improve efficiency, but excessive sharing may facilitate collusion where it didn't exist before. Second-order effects can reduce the efficacy of initiatives implemented to thwart corruption, and may even lead to other kinds of corruption. In addition, many of the new developments in combating corruption, which may be more relevant for cities in the developed world than for cities in emerging nations, may seem appealing until real-world constraints intervene. There is likewise the endemic problem of distinguishing between procurements that are corrupt and those that are merely economically inefficient.

Threading the needle among seemingly conflicting prescriptions may be difficult, especially under the conditions unique to each municipality. Clearly, no one set of remedies will apply across the board. However, mayors ready to tackle procurement as part of a larger assault on systemic corruption arrive at procurement after having first taken the steps outlined in this book, specifically those presented in Box 17. By applying the framework for policy analysis (presented in Box 4) to the city-specific situation, conducting a vulnerability assessment (as suggested in Box 11), designing a systems-focused strategy, and beginning to implement it—perhaps by "frying big fish" or picking "low-hanging fruit"—the municipal leader will have developed important insights into appropriate initiatives for battling corruption in the procurement area, which may already include some low-hanging fruit or harbor a big fish.

In addition, the mayor and other leaders will have begun work streamlining the civil service system—especially the rewards and incentives—to ensure qualified people with the right motivation are in the key procurement slots. In addition, as outlined previously in the narrative, the municipal leaders will have brought enforcement authorities, especially the police, into the team that will tackle corruption in procurement.

Clearly, in extreme situations featuring rampant corruption, weak democratic institutions, and a climate of benign neglect, a municipal leader will not have the luxury to explore the new decentralized discretion idea. More traditional procurement rules and regulations will first be required to bring the system into equilibrium; the costs of bureaucracy are small compared to the potential costs of permitting additional discretion. In this extreme situation, developing a fair, incentive-based, well-understood civil service career system is crucial. Administrative talent is thin, but experiments with developing performance indicators and the incentives linked to them deserve high priority.[25]

Box A1 provides a useful roadmap to help the mayor identify a menu of conventional options tailored to the city's unique situation. Some of the key variables/conditions include:

- **Type of product:** Is the deliverable a piece of hardware, a software package, or a database, something tangible that is handed over to government to complete the contract? Or is the deliverable a service that the vendor performs in behalf of and perhaps under the supervision of the government? The quality features of hardware are usually easier to assess than are those of a service. With a tangible product, a competitive bidding process is more likely to find an equilibrating level.
- **Technology content of deliverable:** Is the product at the leading edge of the technological frontier? Or is it an

everyday, low-tech product like expendables? The uncertainty attendant to technologies that push the envelope of knowledge will inherently nudge companies toward risk aversion, especially on monetarily large contracts. Contracts that preserve clear incentives and avoid the problems of moral hazard are more difficult to craft.

- **Measurability of procurement results/success:** Can the success or failure of the procurement be ascertained straightforwardly, or quantifiably? Or is it inherently qualitative and subjective? The more generic and well understood the product, the better the expected cost and quality can be assessed, and the greater the incentive leverage that can be built into the contract agreement.
- **Frequency of procurement:** Does the municipal government conduct procurements for this item or class of items frequently or infrequently? Frequent procurements make it more possible for conspirators to share information and rotate winning bids over time.
- **Number of potential vendors:** Many or few, perhaps one? Monopoly power is antithetic to the notion of competition.
- **Elasticity of government demand:** Are there substitutes for this product or is it one of a kind? With inelastic demand, providers may have opportunities to price gauge.
- **Civil service career system:** Is the system well-developed, with merit-based upward mobility, and incentive-driven pay and compensation adequate to meet family needs? Or is it poorly specified, longevity-based, with pay and compensation marginal or below the subsistence level, and horizontal equity paramount? A poorly articulated career system, in which employees are paid poorly and

performance has a weak linkage to pay, creates temptations for even the most dedicated public servant; the most talented people will look elsewhere for employment. Reforms in this area are fundamental to preventing corruption, as suggested elsewhere herein.

- **Framework of governance:** Are democratic institutions widespread and effective? Or, are they nonexistent or atrophied? Fair competition cannot flourish in anarchical conditions.
- **Prominence of public sector as an economic actor:** Does the public sector play a relatively small proportionate role in the economic activity of the municipality and the surrounding region? Or, does the public sector dwarf private sector economic activity and employment? Monopsony buying power may breed corruption in the absence of effective controls.

NOTES

Chapter 1

1. Organization for Economic Cooperation and Development (OECD) Symposium on Corruption and Good Governance, Paris, Session 3, March 13–14, 1995, p. 2.

2. Thomas D. Thacher II, "The New York City Construction Authority's Office of the Inspector-General: A Successful New Strategy for Reforming Public Contracting in the Construction Industry," unpublished case study, June 1995.

3. Some literature on corruption in the 1960s tended to excuse corruption as something like a market price when markets weren't allowed or something like an expression of interest when more democratic means were closed. Since then, both empirical and theoretical studies have persuaded most people that most types of corrupt behavior are economically and politically costly, even if they sometimes benefit the group in power. For a review see Robert Klitgaard, *Controlling Corruption* (Berkeley and Los Angeles: University of California Press, 1988), especially pp. 30–48.

4. See Luis Moreno Ocampo, *En Defensa Propia: Cómo Salir de la Corrupción* (Buenos Aires: Editorial Sudamericana, 1993); and Herbert W. Werlin, "Understanding Corruption: Implications for World Bank Staff," unpublished manuscript, August 1994. Another description of generalized corruption is Jean-François Bayart's *L'État en Afrique: La politique du ventre* (Paris: Fayard, 1989).

5. Dipak Gyawali, "Structural Dishonesty: Corruption Culture in Public Works," unpublished manuscript, 1994.

6. John T. Noonan, Jr., *Bribes* (New York: Macmillan, 1985).

7. Audit Commission, *Protecting the Public Purse. Probity in the Public Sector: Combating Fraud and Corruption in Local Government* (London: HMSQ, 1993), p. 3.

8. Claudio Orrego, "Citizen Participation and the Strengthening of Accountability in Chile's Municipal Governments," unpublished manuscript, April 1995, p. 5.

9. The Latin root *corrumpere* refers both to political graft and the seduction of a virgin.

10. Noonan, *Bribes*, pp. 599–600, 701–2.

11. On such cycles in police corruption in the United States, see Lawrence Sherman, *Scandal and Reform* (Berkeley and Los Angeles: University of California Press, 1979), and

Milton Mollen et al., *Commission Report: Commission to Investigate Allegations of Police Corruption and the Anti-Corruption Procedures of the Police Department* (New York: City of New York, July 1994). A theoretical model for the persistence of corruption is presented by Jean Tirole, "Persistence of Corruption," IPR55, Working Paper Series (Washington, D.C.: Institute for Policy Reform, October 1992).

12. Amitai Etzioni, "The Fight against Fraud and Abuse," *Journal of Policy Analysis and Management* 2, no. 4 (Fall 1982).

13. See *Accountability and Transparency in International Economic Development: The Launching of Transparency International in Berlin,* May 1993, ed. Fredrik Galtung (Berlin: German Foundation for International Development and Transparency International, 1994).

Chapter 2

1. Excerpts from *Second Report of the Commission of Enquiry under Sir Alistair Blair-Kerr* (Hong Kong, 1973).

2. Klitgaard, *Controlling Corruption,* p. 100.

3. Frank Anechiarico and James B. Jacobs, *The Pursuit of Absolute Integrity: How Corruption Control Makes Government Ineffective.* Chicago: University of Chicago Press, 1996.

4. For further review of progress in Hong Kong, see Melanie Manion, "Policy Instruments and Political Context: Transforming a Culture of Corruption in Hong Kong," paper presented at the 48th Annual Meeting of the Association for Asian Studies, Honolulu, Hawaii, April 11–14, 1996.

5. The formula is metaphorical in many senses, not least in the notion of addition and subtraction. Corruption is a function of many things, with positive "partial derivatives" with respect to degree of monopoly and to extent of official discretion and a negative partial with respect to accountability. Since each of these variables is multidimensional and since reliable measures are not available, the mathematical metaphor is heuristic only.

Chapter 3

1. Francisco Ramírez Torres, *Los Delitos Económicos en los Negocios* (Managua: Talleres de Don Bosco, 1990), pp. 22–26, 40–50.

Chapter 4 is not annotated.

Chapter 5

1. Which capabilities must be coordinated? Law professor Philip Heymann has outlined ideal preconditions for a campaign against corruption, which may be paraphrased as follows:

Internal Inspection Units. Specialized units with a mix of technical skills, experience, and concentration of effort should be tailored to the unique functional needs of the parent organization.

Specialized Police Units. Law enforcement is essential if anti-corruption cases are to have teeth—that is, if they are enforceable in a court of law. The long-term nature of most anti-corruption investigations, the requirement that information must be usable in a criminal trial, the intrusive and sensitive nature of investigations without a specific victim, and the highly technical nature of modern crime make it highly desirable to educate and train police in anti-corruption methods.

Able, Honest Prosecutors. As the public's champions in the battle against corrupt activities, prosecutors must be skilled and objective in bringing charges against those who would operate outside the laws for personal gain. Often, in the public's eye, the credibility and fairness of the entire political system depend on the prosecutor and his/her team.

Adequate Court Systems. The judicial system is the final arbiter of criminal cases. Especially when "frying big fish," the system must be impartial in its judgments, independent of politics, and effective in trying cases in reasonable time at reasonable cost. (*Source:* Philip Heymann, "Dealing with Corruption: The United States as an Example," unpublished paper, Harvard Law School, 1995.)

To these, we might add a fifth: an *External Inspection Unit.* This organization does not have to be large, only positioned external to and independent from the agency and equipped with interdisciplinary tools to act as an additional brake on corrupt activities.

2. In 1995 Venezuela set up a special anti-corruption office, independent of the coordinating committee, whose apparent function is educational.

3. *De Frente Al Pais: Programa Presidencial de Lucha Contra la Corrupción* (Santafé de Bogotá, Colombia: Presidencia de la República, 1999).

4. Marta Altolaguirre, "Cuando Sucede . . ." *La Prensa* (Guatemala City), Feb. 22, 1990, our translation.

5. Peter Williams, "Concept of an Independent Organisation to Tackle Corruption," paper presented at the International Conference on Corruption and Economic Crime against Government, Washington, D.C., October 1983, p. 23.

6. Heymann, "Dealing with Corruption: The United States as an Example," p. 14.

7. Robert C. Marshall and Michael J. Meurer, "Should Bid Rigging Always Be an Antitrust Violation?" unpublished manuscript, June 1995, p. 59.

8. Excerpted from Klitgaard's interview with Plana in 1982.

Chapter 6

1. "Los paceños ya no creen en nadie," *Ultima Hora* special report, Feb. 18, 1996, pp. 18–19. The poll was taken using an age-stratified random sample of adults from 18 to 65 years old from the four zones of the city "and of the middle class." The sample size was not indicated.

2. *The Asian Wall Street Journal,* June 11, 1996, cited in *Business Day,* June 12, 1996, p. 12.

3. Eugene Linden, "The Exploding Cities of the Developing World," *Foreign Affairs* 75, no. 1 (January–February 1996): 63.

4. Bernardino Bravo, "Democracia: ¿Antídoto frente a la corrupción?" *Estudios Políticos,* no. 52 (Primavera 1993): 299–308.

5. See Robert Klitgaard, "Information and Incentives in Institutional Reform," in Christopher Clague, ed., *Institutions and Economic Development* (Baltimore: Johns Hopkins University Press, 1997); and Robert Klitgaard, "Institutional Adjustment and Adjusting to Institutions," Discussion Paper no. 303 (Washington, D.C.: The World Bank, September 1995). Performance-based pay and promotion also benefit from a significant national effort to develop appropriate measures and safeguards, as recent advances in the United States and other OECD countries indicate. Sometimes civil service regulations must be changed or bypassed through experiments, when they constrain the use of performance-related pay.

Appendix

1. The first set of mismatches may occur between the procuring official and government if the procuring official has system-driven or personal incentives to make decisions that do not maximize the public's welfare. A single-minded focus on either cost (pick the low bidder, especially if quality differences are difficult to assess) or quality (seek the highest-quality products, with cost a distant consideration—sometimes the case with some defense weapons system acquisitions) may favor specific vendors. Procurement officials themselves may reflect different biases, the contracting officers inherently focusing on cost and the technical advisers on quality. At times, procurement officials may exhibit firm-specific favoritism for reasons other than a direct bribe or kickback (for example, to set the stage for a future employment opportunity). Finally, the so-called "appropriability" problem recognizes the mismatch between the risks borne by procurement officials and the rewards they may receive for conducting an efficient, surplus-maximizing contract. This not only may lead to too little effort by the official but may open the door to corruption temptations.

2. See, for example, Johannes Fedderke and Robert Klitgaard, "Economic Growth and Social Indicators: An Exploratory Analysis," *Economic Development and Cultural Change* 46, no. 3 (April 1998), and the references therein.

3. See John McLaren, "Supplier Relations and the Market Context: A Theory of Handshakes," Center Discussion Paper no. 766 (New Haven: Economic Growth Center, Yale University, October 1996), and the references therein.

4. See "Box 13: An Independent Office to Fight Corruption in New York City's School Construction" and the later discussion of effective municipal use of an elaborate bidder prequalification process to screen potential bidders on past performance.

5. See Klitgaard, *Controlling Corruption*, Chapter 7, for a discussion of contracting between the U.S. Army and South Korean–owned firms.

6. The recent experience of the U.S. Navy's A-12 Stealth Fighter, the largest-ever major weapons contract cancellation by the U.S. Department of Defense, may have been at least partially attributable to this phenomenon. Though a federal judge is expected to award the contractors damages, the U.S. Department of Justice has appealed the case.

7. If bidders each know something about the "true" costs and risks but know different things, then by sharing their information they will make more socially efficient

bids. The downside, of course, is the possibility that such sharing leads to collusive bidding, which will seldom be socially efficient. The point is that a trade-off exists that is not recognized in the traditional preference for no sharing at all.

8. For one discussion of this process, see Robert C. Marshall, Michael J. Meurer, and Jean-François Richard, "Incentive-Based Procurement Oversight by Protest," in J. Leitzel, and J. Tirole, eds., *Incentives in Procurement Contracting* (Boulder, Colo.: Westview Press, 1993). See also Steven Kelman, *Procurement and Public Management* (Washington, D.C.: AEI Press, 1990), especially pp. 23–24.

9. The principle is derived and discussed in Paul Milgrom and John Roberts, *Economics, Organization and Management* (Englewood Cliffs, N.J.: Prentice-Hall, 1992). The empirical evidence on performance-based pay, especially in the private sector, is summarized in Alan S. Blinder, ed., *Paying for Productivity: A Look at the Evidence* (Washington, D.C.: The Brookings Institution, 1990).

10. Klitgaard, "Information and Incentives in Institutional Reform," shows that when the measurement of performance improves, a wage package can be constructed that both enhances incentives and reduces risk. He also notes the limits to optimal incentive theory once dynamic considerations and real-world practicalities are taken into consideration. In their remarkable theoretical treatment, Jean-Jacques Laffont and Jean Tirole note that optimal linear incentive schemes "were no longer so once dynamics, political economy, or multi-principal conditions were thrown in." See *A Theory of Incentives in Procurement and Regulation* (Cambridge, Mass.: MIT Press, 1993), p. 663.

11. Robert Klitgaard, "Institutional Adjustment and Adjusting to Institutions."

12. Thomas D. Thacher, II, "The New York City Construction Authority's . . ."

13. Robert H. Porter and Douglas J. Zona, "Detection of Bid Rigging in Procurement Auctions," *Journal of Political Economy*. 101, no. 3 (1993). Though the model used *ex post* information to show that the variance of cartel bids on individual contracts was smaller than the distribution of bids from "competitive" bidders, excursions of the model could examine selected combinations of firms suspected of engaging in collusive bidding, or could examine all combinations. As the authors point out, it is sometimes difficult to distinguish between collusive and competitive equilibrium situations because both depend on the rules of the procurement process and the economic environment.

14. Riordan and Sappington demonstrate theoretically that sole sourcing should be preferred to second sourcing *ex ante* over a wide range of conditions. Their simulations show that sole sourcing is "more likely to be preferred: (a) the more rapidly the prototype (for example, a weapons system) becomes obsolete; (b) the longer is the expected development lag; (c) the less highly future benefits are discounted; and (d) the greater the likelihood of cost overruns." See Michael H. Riordan and David E. M. Sappington, "Second Sourcing," *RAND Journal of Economics* 20, no. 1, Spring 1989, p. 42. For related discussion, see Michael H. Riordan, "Incentives for Cost Reduction in Defense Procurement," in J. Leitzel and J. Tirole, eds., *Incentives in Procurement Contracting* (Boulder, Colo.: Westview Press, 1993).

15. Mollen et al, Commission Report (fn. 10 supra).

16. Gyawali, "Structural Dishonesty: Corruption Culture in Public Works."

17. Kelman, *Procurement and Public Management.*

18. More generally, different forms of procurement contracts create their own second-order problems. Fixed-cost contracts put all the risk on the contractor, which affects bid prices adversely; at the other extreme, cost-plus contracts enable cost-inflating incentives. Risk-sharing contracts come in many forms (fixed price incentive contracts, for example, find procurer and vendor sharing costs above a certain level, perhaps up to but not exceeding another level) and have intermediate effects, moral hazard being one. However, there is an economically "optimal" amount of risk inherent in any contract.

19. Heymann. "Dealing with Corruption," 1995, p. 6.

20. Kelman, *Procurement and Public Management,* p. 22.

21. Kelman, *Procurement and Public Management,* p. 121.

22. Marshall et al., "Incentive-Based Procurement Oversight by Protest."

23. Marshall et al., "Incentive-Based Procurement Oversight by Protest," p. 51.

24. Kelman, *Procurement and Public Management,* cites an out-of-court settlement in which the loser of the initial competition was selected as the winning vendor, supplying the exact solution and hardware the winner of the initial competition had bid. Subsequently, the government agency ultimately paid much higher prices for the equipment than they would have under the initial contract, though the total present value price of the contract did not change. (See Case Study 3, pp. 132–42). As a consequence of this, Marshall et al. argue that all types of settlements between firms should be banned because "[i]nterfirm settlements . . . produce outcomes that are exactly equivalent to those that would be attained through explicit collusion between the firms." Robert C. Marshall, Michael J. Meurer, and Jean-François Richard, "Curbing Agency Problems in the Procurement Process by Protest Oversight," *RAND Journal of Economics* 25, no. 2, Summer 1994, p. 298.

25. Robert Klitgaard, "Healing Sick Institutions," in Silvio Borner and Martin Paldam, ed., *The Political Dimension in Economic Growth.* (London: Macmillan, 1997).

Index

The Authors

Robert Klitgaard, Dean and Ford Distinguished Professor of International Development and Security at the RAND Graduate School in Santa Monica, California; former professor at Yale's School of Management, Harvard's Kennedy School of Government, and the University of Natal; a consultant, with experience in twenty-seven developing countries, to the White House, the World Bank, the International Monetary Fund, the U.S. Agency for International Development, the United Nations Development Program, the Organization for Economic Cooperation and Development, and the Rockefeller and Ford foundations; and author of six other books including *Controlling Corruption* and *Tropical Gangsters,* which the editors of the *New York Times Book Review* named one of the six best nonfiction books of 1990.

Ronald MacLean-Abaroa, four-time elected mayor of La Paz, making him the longest democratically tenured mayor in Bolivia's history; minister of planning and foreign minister of Bolivia; manager of successful private companies and his own consulting firm; and a founding member of Transparency International and its first president for Latin America.

H. Lindsey Parris, management consultant on matters of organizational reform, including a recent study of innovation and creativity in large organizations; and retired U.S. Air Force colonel who managed aspects of the Strategic Defense Initiative and served on the staff of the National Defense University.